Chartered Institute of
anagement Accountants

How to access your on-line resources

Kaplan Financial students will have a MyKaplan account and these extra resources will be available to you online. You do not need to register again, as this process was completed when you enrolled. If you are having problems accessing online materials, please ask your course administrator.

If you are not studying with Kaplan and did not purchase your book via a Kaplan website, to unlock your extra online resources please go to www.en-gage.co.uk (even if you have set up an account and registered books previously). You will then need to enter the ISBN number (on the title page and back cover) and the unique pass key number contained in the scratch panel below to gain access.

You will also be required to enter additional information during this process to set up or confirm your account details.

If you purchased through Kaplan Flexible Learning or via the Kaplan Publishing website you will automatically receive an e-mail invitation to register your details and gain access to your content. If you do not receive the e-mail or book content, please contact Kaplan Publishing.

Your code and information

This code can only be used once for the registration of one book online. This registration and your online content will expire when the final sittings for the examinations covered by this book have taken place. Please allow one hour from the time you submit your book details for us to process your request.

Please scratch the film to access your unique code.

Please be aware that this code is case-sensitive and you will need to include the dashes within the passcode, but not when entering the ISBN.

Managerial Level

Subject E2

Project and Relationship Management

EXAM PRACTICE KIT

Published by: Kaplan Publishing UK

Unit 2 The Business Centre, Molly Millars Lane, Wokingham, Berkshire RG41 2QZ

Notice

British Library Cataloguing in Publication Data

A catalogue record for this book is available from the British Library

ISBN: 978-1-78415-933-7

Printed and bound in Great Britain

CONTENTS

Section

Quality and accuracy are of the utmost importance to us so if you spot an error in any of our products, please send an email to mykaplanreporting@kaplan.com with full details.

Our Quality Co-ordinator will work with our technical team to verify the error and take action to ensure it is corrected in future editions.

INDEX TO QUESTIONS AND ANSWERS

OBJECTIVE TEST QUESTIONS

EXAM TECHNIQUES

COMPUTER-BASED ASSESSMENT

TEN GOLDEN RULES

1   Make sure you have completed the compulsory 15 minute tutorial before you start exam. This tutorial is available through the CIMA website. You cannot speak to the invigilator once you have started.

2   These exam practice kits give you plenty of exam style questions to practise so make sure you use them to fully prepare.

3   Attempt all questions, there is no negative marking.

4   Double check your answer before you put in the final answer although you can change your response as many times as you like.

5   On multiple choice questions (MCQs), there is only one correct answer.

6   Not all questions will be MCQs – you may have to fill in missing words or figures.

7   Identify the easy questions first and get some points on the board to build up your confidence.

8   Try and allow 15 minutes at the end to check your answers and make any corrections.

9   If you don't know the answer, flag the question and attempt it later. In your final review before the end of the exam try a process of elimination.

10 Work out your answer on the whiteboard provided first if it is easier for you. There is also an on-screen 'scratch pad' on which you can make notes. You are not allowed to take pens, pencils, rulers, pencil cases, phones, paper or notes.

SYLLABUS GUIDANCE, LEARNING OBJECTIVES AND VERBS

A AIMS OF THE SYLLABUS

The aims of the syllabus are

- to provide for the Institute, together with the practical experience requirements, an adequate basis for assuring society that those admitted to membership are competent to act as management accountants for entities, whether in manufacturing, commercial or service organisations, in the public or private sectors of the economy
- to enable the Institute to examine whether prospective members have an adequate knowledge, understanding and mastery of the stated body of knowledge and skills
- to complement the Institute's practical experience and skills development requirements.

B STUDY WEIGHTINGS

A percentage weighting is shown against each topic in the syllabus. This is intended as a guide to the proportion of study time each topic requires.

All component learning outcomes will be tested and one question may cover more than one component learning outcome.

The weightings do not specify the number of marks that will be allocated to topics in the examination.

C LEARNING OUTCOMES

Each topic within the syllabus contains a list of learning outcomes, which should be read in conjunction with the knowledge content for the syllabus. A learning outcome has two main purposes:

1   to define the skill or ability that a well-prepared candidate should be able to exhibit in the examination

2   to demonstrate the approach likely to be taken by examiners in examination questions.

The learning outcomes are part of a hierarchy of learning objectives. The verbs used at the beginning of each learning outcome relate to a specific learning objective, e.g. Evaluate alternative approaches to budgeting.

The verb 'evaluate' indicates a high-level learning objective. As learning objectives are hierarchical, it is expected that at this level students will have knowledge of different budgeting systems and methodologies and be able to apply them.

A list of the learning objectives and the verbs that appear in the syllabus learning outcomes and examinations follows and these will help you to understand the depth and breadth required for a topic and the skill level the topic relates to.

Learning objectives	Verbs used	Definition
1 Knowledge		
What you are expected to know	List	Make a list of
	State	Express, fully or clearly, the details of/facts of
	Define	Give the exact meaning of
2 Comprehension		
What you are expected to understand	Describe	Communicate the key features of
	Distinguish	Highlight the differences between
	Explain	Make clear or intelligible/State the meaning of
	Identify	Recognise, establish or select after consideration
	Illustrate	Use an example to describe or explain something
3 Application		
How you are expected to apply your knowledge	Apply	To put to practical use
	Calculate/compute	To ascertain or reckon mathematically
	Demonstrate	To prove with certainty or to exhibit by practical means
	Prepare	To make or get ready for use
	Reconcile	To make or prove consistent/compatible
	Solve	Find an answer to
	Tabulate	Arrange in a table
4 Analysis		
How you are expected to analyse the detail of what you have learned	Analyse	Examine in detail the structure of
	Categorise	Place into a defined class or division
	Compare and contrast	Show the similarities and/or differences between
	Construct	To build up or compile
	Discuss	To examine in detail by argument
	Interpret	To translate into intelligible or familiar terms
	Produce	To create or bring into existence
5 Evaluation		
How you are expected to use your learning to evaluate, make decisions or recommendations	Advise	To counsel, inform or notify
	Evaluate	To appraise or assess the value of
	Recommend	To advise on a course of action
	Advise	To counsel, inform or notify

D OBJECTIVE TEST

The most common types of Objective Test questions are:

- multiple choice, where you have to choose the correct answer(s) from a list of possible answers. This could either be numbers or text.

- multiple choice with more choices and answers – for example, choosing two correct answers from a list of eight possible answers. This could either be numbers or text.

- single numeric entry, where you give your numeric answer e.g. profit is $10,000.

- multiple entry, where you give several numeric answers e.g. the charge for electricity is $2000 and the accrual is $200.

- true/false questions, where you state whether a statement is true or false e.g. external auditors report to the directors is FALSE.

- matching pairs of text e.g. the convention 'prudence' would be matched with the statement' inventories revalued at the lower of cost and net realisable value'.

- other types could be matching text with graphs and labelling graphs/diagrams.

In this Exam Practice Kit we have used these types of questions.

Some further guidance from CIMA on number entry questions is as follows:

- For number entry questions, you do not need to include currency symbols or other characters or symbols such as the percentage sign, as these will have been completed for you. You may use the decimal point but must not use any other characters when entering an answer (except numbers) so, for example, $10,500.80 would be input as 10500.80

- When expressing a decimal, for example a probability or correlation coefficient, you should include the leading zero (i.e. you should input 0.5 not .5)

- Negative numbers should be input using the minus sign, for example –1000

- You will receive an error message if you try to enter a character or symbol that is not permitted (for example a '£' or '%' sign)

- A small range of answers will normally be accepted, taking into account sensible rounding

Guidance re CIMA On-Screen calculator:

As part of the computer based assessment software, candidates are now provided with a calculator. This calculator is on-screen and is available for the duration of the assessment. The calculator is accessed by clicking the calculator button in the top left hand corner of the screen at any time during the assessment.

All candidates must complete a 15 minute tutorial before the assessment begins and will have the opportunity to familiarise themselves with the calculator and practise using it.

Candidates may practise using the calculator by downloading and installing the practice exam at http://www.vue.com/athena/. The calculator can be accessed from the fourth sample question (of 12).

Please note that the practice exam and tutorial provided by Pearson VUE at http://www.vue.com/athena/ is not specific to CIMA and includes the full range of question types the Pearson VUE software supports, some of which CIMA does not currently use.

The Objective Tests are ninety minute computer-based assessments comprising 60 compulsory questions, with one or more parts. CIMA is continuously developing the question styles within the system and you are advised to try the online website demo at www.cimaglobal.com, to both gain familiarity with assessment software and examine the latest style of questions being used.

APPROACH TO REVISION

Stage 1: Assess areas of strengths and weaknesses

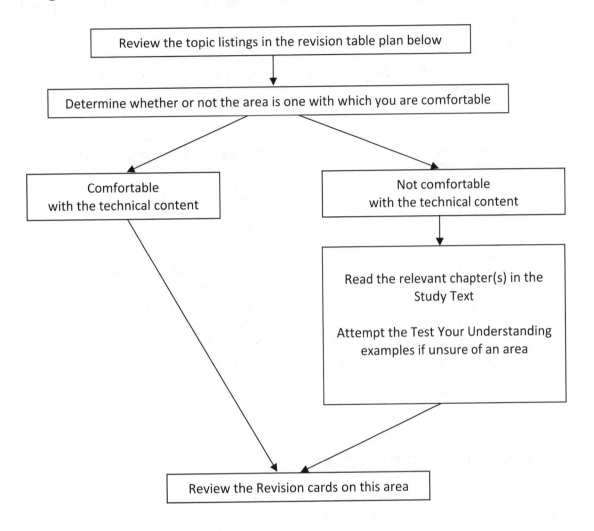

Review the topic listings in the revision table plan below

Determine whether or not the area is one with which you are comfortable

Comfortable
with the technical content

Not comfortable
with the technical content

Read the relevant chapter(s) in the
Study Text

Attempt the Test Your Understanding
examples if unsure of an area

Review the Revision cards on this area

Stage 2: Question practice

Follow the order of revision of topics as recommended in the revision table plan below and attempt the questions in the order suggested.

Try to avoid referring to text books and notes and the model answer until you have completed your attempt.

Try to answer the question in the allotted time.

Review your attempt with the model answer and assess how much of the answer you achieved in the allocated exam time.

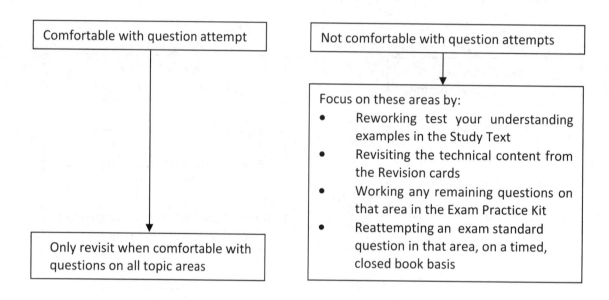

Stage 3: Final pre-exam revision

We recommend that you **attempt at least one ninety minute mock examination** containing a set of previously unseen exam standard questions.

It is important that you get a feel for the breadth of coverage of a real exam without advanced knowledge of the topic areas covered – just as you will expect to see on the real exam day.

Ideally a mock examination offered by your tuition provider should be sat in timed, closed book, real exam conditions.

E2
PROJECT AND RELATIONSHIP MANAGEMENT

Syllabus overview

E2 emphasises a holistic, integrated approach to managing organisations, from external and internal perspectives. It builds on the understanding of organisational structuring gained from E1 and is centred on the concept of strategy and how organisational strategy can be implemented through people, projects, processes and relationships. It provides the basis for developing further insights into how to formulate and implement organisational strategy, which is covered in E3.

Summary of syllabus

Weight	Syllabus topic
30%	A. Introduction to strategic management and assessing the global environment
20%	B. The human aspects of the organisation
20%	C. Managing relationships
30%	D. Managing change through projects

E2 – A. INTRODUCTION TO STRATEGIC MANAGEMENT ASSESSING THE GLOBAL ENVIRONMENT (30%)

Learning outcomes
On completion of their studies, students should be able to:

Lead	Component	Indicative syllabus content
1 discuss developments in strategic management.	(a) discuss the concept of strategy and the rational/formal approach to strategy development	• Defining strategy and strategic management. • Core areas of strategic management. • Levels of strategy within organisations. • Stages in the rational approach to strategy developments.
	(b) compare and contrast alternative approaches to strategy development	• Intended, emergent, logical incrementalism, and political approaches. • Resource-based view – resources and competencies, internal value and dynamic capabilities. • Strategy development in different contexts, e.g. SMEs, public sector, not-for-profit. • Strategy and structure.
	(c) explain the approaches to achieving sustainable competitive advantage.	• The concept of competitive advantage. • Generic competitive strategies. • Value, rarity, inimitability, non-substitutability as bases of competitive advantage. • Achieving sustainable competitive advantage.
2 analyse the relationship between different aspects of the global business environment.	(a) distinguish between different aspects of the global business environment, including the competitive environment	• The macro and micro environments. • LoNGPEST analysis and its derivatives. • Globalisation. • Country and political risk factors. • Emerging markets. • Porter's Diamond and its use for assessing the competitive advantage of nations. • Porter's Five Forces model and its use for analysing the external environment.

Learning outcomes

On completion of their studies, students should be able to:

Lead	Component	Indicative syllabus content
	(b) discuss the approaches to competitor analysis including the collection and interpretation of trend data.	• Key concepts in competitor analysis. • The role of competitor analysis. • Approaches to collecting competitor information. • Sources, types and quality of competitor data. • Analysing and interpreting competitor data. • The application of Big Data to competitor analysis.

E2 – B. THE HUMAN ASPECTS OF THE ORGANISATION (20%)

Learning outcomes
On completion of their studies, students should be able to:

Lead	Component	Indicative syllabus content
1 discuss the concepts associated with managing through people.	(a) discuss the concepts of leadership and management	<ul><li>Fundamental and contemporary concepts in management.</li><li>The concepts of power, authority, delegation and empowerment.</li><li>Different approaches to leadership, including personality/traits, style, contingency/situation, transactional/transformational, distributive.</li><li>Leadership in different contexts.</li></ul>
	(b) discuss HRM approaches for managing and controlling individuals' performance.	<ul><li>HR policies and procedures.</li><li>Different approaches to employee performance appraisals.</li><li>The contribution of coaching and mentoring in enhancing individual and organisational performance.</li><li>Equality and diversity practices.</li><li>Disciplinary and grievance procedures in resolving poor performance.</li><li>Dismissal and redundancy.</li><li>Employer and employee responsibilities in managing the work environment (e.g. health and safety).</li></ul>
2 discuss the hard and soft aspects of people and organisational performance.	(a) discuss behavioural aspects of management control	<ul><li>Theories of behavioural aspects of control.</li><li>Performance management and measurement frameworks, e.g.<ul><li>– target setting</li><li>– management by objectives</li><li>– the Balanced Scorecard (BSC).</li></ul></li><li>Trust and control.</li></ul>

Learning outcomes

On completion of their studies, students should be able to:

Lead	Component	Indicative syllabus content
	(b) explain the importance of organisational culture.	<ul><li>Explaining the concept and importance of culture.</li><li>Levels of culture.</li><li>Influences on culture.</li><li>Analysing organisational culture – the cultural web framework.</li><li>Models for categorising culture.</li><li>National cultures and managing in different cultures.</li></ul>

E2 – C. MANAGING RELATIONSHIPS (20%)

Learning outcomes
On completion of their studies, students should be able to:

Lead	Component		Indicative syllabus content
1 discuss the effectiveness of organisational relationships.	(a)	evaluate the issues associated with building, leading and managing effective teams	• Building effective and high-performing teams. • Leading and managing teams. • Factors associated with effective team work. • Motivating team members. • Resolving problems and conflict in teams.
	(b)	discuss the effectiveness of handling relationships between the finance function and other parts of the organisation and the supply chain	• Management of relationships between the finance function and other parts of the organisation (internal). • The concept of the Chartered Management Accountant as a business partner in creating value. • Transaction cost theory in the context of shared service centres and outsourcing, including contractual relationship, SLAs (service level agreements), bounded rationality and co-creation with customers.
	(c)	discuss the effectiveness of handling relationships between the finance function and external experts and stakeholders.	• Management of relationships with professional advisors (external) e.g. accounting, tax and legal, auditors and financial stakeholders such as shareholders and other investors to meet organisational objectives and governance responsibilities.
2 discuss management tools and techniques in managing organisational relationships.	(a)	discuss the roles of communication, negotiation, influence and persuasion in the management process	• The communication process, types of communication tools and their use, ways of managing communication problems. • The importance of effective communication skills for the Chartered Management Accountant. • The importance of non-verbal communication and feedback. • Developing effective strategies for influence/persuasion/negotiation. • The process of negotiation. • Negotiation skills.

Learning outcomes
On completion of their studies, students should be able to:

Lead	Component	Indicative syllabus content
	(b) discuss approaches to managing conflict.	• The sources and causes of conflict in organisations. • The different forms and types of conflict. • Strategies for managing conflict to ensure working relationships are productive and effective.

E2 – D. MANAGING CHANGE THROUGH PROJECTS (30%)

Learning outcomes
On completion of their studies, students should be able to:

Lead	Component	Indicative syllabus content
1 advise on important elements in the change process.	(a) discuss the concept of organisational change	• Types of change. • External and internal triggers for change. • Stage model of change management. • Principles of change management.
	(b) recommend techniques to manage resistance to change.	• Problem identification as a precursor to change. • Reasons for resistance to change. • Approaches to managing resistance to change.
2 discuss the concepts involved in managing projects.	(a) discuss the characteristics of the different phases of a project	• Definition of project attributes. • Time, cost and quality project objectives. • The purpose and activities associated with the key stages in the project lifecycle. • Examples of the role of project management methodologies in project control (e.g. PRINCE2, PMI).
	(b) apply tools and techniques for project managers	• Key tools for project management, including work breakdown schedule (WBS), Gantt Charts, and Network analysis. • Managing project risk. • PERT charts. • Scenario planning and buffering. • The contribution of project management software.
	(c) discuss management and leadership issues associated with projects, including the roles of key players in projects.	• Project structures, including matrix structure and their impact on project achievement. • The role and attributes of an effective project manager. • The role of the Chartered Management Accountant in projects. • The role of other key players in a project. • Managing key project stakeholders. • The lifecycle of project teams. • Leading and motivating project teams.

FORMULAE AND TABLES

Information concerning formulae and tables will be provided via the CIMA website, www.cimaglobal.com, and your ENgage login.

Section 1

OBJECTIVE TEST QUESTIONS

STRATEGIC MANAGEMENT AND THE GLOBAL ENVIRONMENT

1   According to Drucker, there are five fundamental questions which organisations should consider when setting its strategy. Which of the following are Drucker's fundamental questions? Select all that apply.

    A   What is our mission?

    B   How will we compete in our chosen industry?

    C   What is valued by our customer?

    D   What is our plan?

    E   What should our business be?

    F   What is our vision?

2   Those things which must go right if the objectives and goals of an organisation are to be achieved are known as which of the following?

    A   Key performance indicators

    B   Performance targets

    C   Operational objectives

    D   Critical success factors

3   Which of the following are techniques suggested by Cyert and March for resolving stakeholder conflict? Select all that apply.

    A   Sequential attention

    B   Keep informed

    C   Weighting and scoring

    D   Satisficing

    E   Side payments

    F   Prioritisation

4   **Cultural or demographic factors would generally be considered under which heading in the PESTLE framework?**

  • Political

  • Economic

  • Social

  • Technological

  • Legal

  • Environmental

5   The following diagram depicting the rational/formal model of strategy formulation has several gaps.

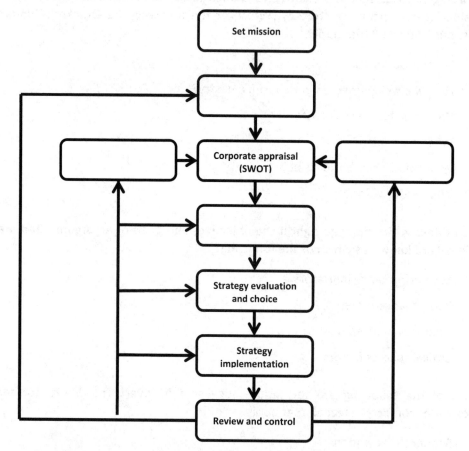

Complete the gaps by dragging the correct word to the correct place on the diagram.

External analysis	Stakeholder analysis	Internal analysis

Establish objectives	Generate strategy options	Competitor review

6   K is a successful entrepreneur. He is considering entering a new market which he considers will generate profits of over $30,000 per annum. He has discovered that to set up the new business he would have to purchase a machine costing $18,000, purchase a licence costing $3,000 and attend an intensive two day training course.

Which of the following situations would Porter's five forces model suggest?

A   The power of the supplier is low

B   Rivalry is high

C   The threat of new entrants is high

D   The power of buyers is low

7   Ansoff's matrix suggests the following four alternatives which organisations can adopt when considering strategic direction.

| Market penetration |
| Product development |
| Diversification |
| Market development |

Complete Ansoff's Matrix by placing the correct strategy in the correct space on the matrix.

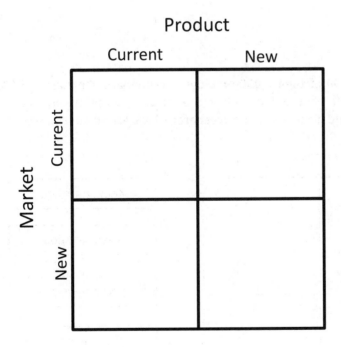

8   PQR manufactures cardboard packaging. It is considering moving into the plastic packaging market. It has established that there are four main plastic packaging manufacturers, who have an aggregate market share of 82%. The current market leader has a share of 26%. The four companies produce products of similar size and quality. The market for plastic packaging has grown by 2% per annum in recent years.

Identify which aspect of Porter's five forces would consider this information and identify if the scenario suggests that the force would be high or low.

New entrant
Power of buyer
Power of supplier
Substitutes
Rivalry

Low
High

The force which would consider this information is _____ and from the scenario, the force would be _____.

9   **There are four main ways in which an organisation can react to environmental situations. Where an organisation recognises an environmental problem but has decided it will be insignificant and have a short-term implication, its likely reaction would be:**

A   Introduce internal controls

B   Plan major strategic change

C   Do nothing

D   Increase its flexibility

10   **ABC is considering making 200 of their 3,000 employees redundant. Only around 2% of ABC's workers are members of a union. Select the most appropriate management strategy for the employees and place it in the correct area of the Mendelow matrix.**

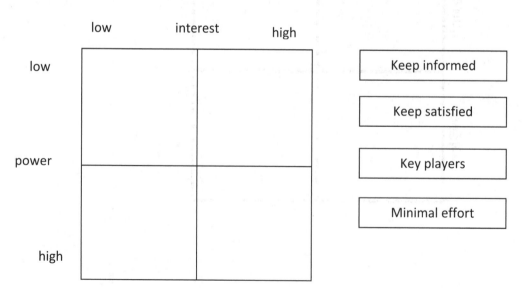

11   Which TWO of the following would generally be accepted as contributing towards globalisation?

A   Liberalisation of trade

B   Increased government regulation

C   Developments in communication networks

D   Increasing concern for environmental issues

E   Developments in employment legislation

12   Drag the elements of the emergent approach on to the correct place on the diagram.

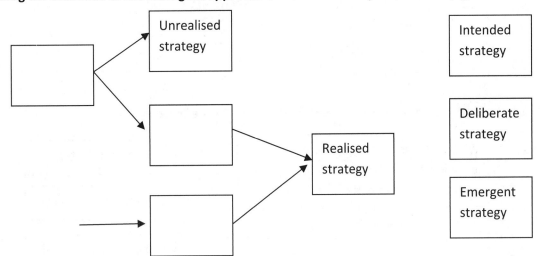

13   Availability of raw materials would come under which heading in Porter's diamond model?

A   Related and supporting industries

B   Factor conditions

C   Firm strategy, structure and rivalry

D   Demand conditions

14   Insert the correct words to complete the sentences about research.

Qualitative	Ratios	Strategic benchmarks
Trend	Quantitative	Focus groups

_____ research involves the collection of non-numerical data. It investigates the WHY decisions that consumers make. _____ research involves gathering factual and numerical data which can then be analysed using _____ analysis or _____.

15 **According to Porter's diamond model which of the following would NOT enhance the demand conditions?**

A   Customers being innovative with their purchasing behaviour

B   Products being slow to reach the maturity stage

C   A varied customer based allowing segmentation

D   Demanding and critical customers

16 **In Porter's five forces model, which of the following is NOT a barrier to entry?**

A   Economies of scale

B   Switching costs

C   Numerous suppliers

D   Product differentiation

17 **Select the correct term for each of the following definitions:**

Strategies which can arise as a result of developing a strategy but changing it in light of new and better opportunities.	Imposed strategy
	Unrealised strategy
Strategies which involve taking small steps towards the desired outcome.	Opportunistic strategy
	Emergent strategy
Strategies which are forced on the organisation by circumstances	Incremental strategy

18 According to Mendelow, the significance of each stakeholder group in an organisation depends on two factors: the power of the stakeholder and the level of interest of the stakeholder.

Interest

Power		Low	High
	Low	I	II
	High	III	IV

What approach is recommended for dealing with stakeholders in quadrant III of the above matrix?

A   Develop strategies that are fully acceptable to the stakeholder

B   Keep the stakeholder satisfied

C   Keep the stakeholder informed

D   Minimum effort

19 BCD is undertaking a corporate appraisal as part of its development of a new strategy. Its analysis has discovered the following:

- Its staff are expert in their industry and no other company has the level of knowledge and experience that BCD has.

- The key raw material required for its product is only available from one main supplier.

- Customers value the high level of after sales care they receive from BCD.

- The government of the country where BCD operates is planning to introduce a tax on the type of products which BCD manufactures.

Match these findings to the technique which BCD would have used in discovering it as part of its corporate appraisal.

A PESTLE

B Porter's five forces

C Resource audit

D Porter's value chain

20 **Porter identified nine 'value activities' in an organisation, which he divided into primary activities and support activities. Which of the following is a primary activity?**

A Procurement

B Technology development

C Human resource management

D Service

21 **Porter's work on industry competition suggests that the strength of market entry depends on the existence of barriers to entry. Identify THREE factors that create barriers to entering an industry.**

A Economies of scale

B Capital requirements

C Expanding market

D Vertical integration

E Many small competitors

22 **In a multi-divisional organisation which produces a range of products for different markets, the business level strategy of each unit or division is mainly concerned with which of the following?**

A setting the direction for the organisation

B the competitiveness of a particular division

C the efficiency of production, marketing and other functions

D alignment of strategy with other organisations

23 There are some key concepts which are helpful when undertaking competitor analysis. These concepts involve gaining an understanding of market share, market size and market growth. Match the definition to the correct term.

Market share	The number of individuals in a certain market who are potential buyers and/or sellers of a product or service.
Market size	The increase in the demand for a particular product or service over time.
Market growth	The portion of a market controlled by a particular company or product.

24 Corporate appraisal involves which of the following?

A evaluating strategic options

B communicating the mission

C identifying strengths and weaknesses

D implementing strategy.

25 Which TWO of the following are advantages of the rational/formal planning approach to strategy formulation?

A It ensures that the whole organisation is working towards the same goals

B It allows the organisation to respond quickly to change in the environment

C It sets clear targets enabling the success of the strategy to be reviewed

D It is useful when the environment is experiencing dynamic change

E It is suitable for use in all organisations.

26 Match the following to the level within the organisation at which the decision would occur.

• Decisions about acquisitions, mergers and sell-offs

• Decisions about what products should be developed

• Decisions about how to gain competitive advantage

• Decisions about how integrated the business should be

• Decisions about how to run the business on a day-to-day basis

| Functional level | Corporate level | Business level |

27 Identify the approach to strategy which proposes that competitive advantage is achieved from the organisation's unique assets or core competences.

A Positioning approach

B Emergent

C Incrementalism

D Resource-based view

28 Strategic objectives have particular criteria that differentiate them from aims or goals. Which TWO of the following criteria relate to objectives?

A   A specific target

B   Should be acceptable

C   Realistic

D   Not time constrained

E   Measurable

29 According to Ansoff's matrix, an organisation that seeks to maintain or increase share of an existing market with an existing product is following which of the following strategies?

A   Market development

B   Diversification

C   Market penetration

D   Product development

30 WXY runs a chain of bars and night clubs within country H. It is considering extending its operations to neighbouring countries. Match up the following macro-economic factors with the heading they would be analysed under in a PESTLE analysis.

Political	Economic	Social	Technological	Legal	Environmental

The age at which people are allowed to drink alcohol
Government tax on sales of alcohol
The level of disposable income people have
People's religious beliefs and attitudes towards alcohol

31 Objectives in a not-for-profit are referred to as the three Es. What are the three Es?

A   Effectiveness, Economy, Efficiency

B   Effectiveness, Environmental, Economy

C   Ecological, Equality, Effectiveness

D   Ecological, Economy, Efficiency

32 According to Porter, there are three generic strategies through which an organisation can gain competitive advantage. What are the three generic strategies?

A   Cost leadership, Differentiation, Focus

B   Market Penetration, Diversification, Product Development

C   Internal development, Strategic alliances, Takeovers and mergers

D   Corporate, Business, Operational

33   **Objectives are often said to be SMART. What does SMART stand for?**

   A   Specific, Manageable, Accountable, Relevant, Tactical

   B   Specific, Measureable, Achievable, Relevant, Timely

   C   Scientific, Measureable, Achievable, Realistic, Tactical

   D   Specific, Measureable, Authoritative, Responsible, Timely

34   **Country L is home to a large number of successful international fashion brands, specialising in handbags. Porter's Diamond seeks to explain the reasons for this. Which TWO of the following would be a factor analysed under related and supporting industries?**

   A   A large number of locally skilled fashion designers

   B   The existence of world renowned fashion shows in Country L

   C   Customers that are particularly fashion conscious

   D   A history of intense competition domestically

   E   Presence of a large number of leather working plants

35   **Which THREE of the following are ways in which Mintzberg defines strategy?**

   A   Strategy as Ploy

   B   Strategy as Plot

   C   Strategy as Position

   D   Strategy as Perspective

   E   Strategy as Persistence

   F   Strategy as Potential

36   **Kotler identified four levels of competitors. Match each level with its explanation.**

Brand competitors	Suppliers whose products satisfy the same needs although they are technically quite different.
Industry competitors	Competitors who compete for the same income.
Form competitors	Suppliers who produce similar goods but are not necessarily the same size or structure.
Generic competitors	Companies which offer similar products with similar prices.

37   **A strategy whereby the organisation has a clear view of where it wants to go, but it then proceeds towards this goal using small steps, adapting to environmental changes along the way is known as which of the following?**

   A   Freewheeling opportunism

   B   Logical incrementalism

   C   Muddling through

   D   Emergent strategy

38 **Which of the following is NOT one of the purposes of qualitative research?**

A   To discover the existence of opinions

B   To measure the 'amount' of opinion

C   To indicate different viewpoints

D   To gather unexpected data

39 BCD is a large trading company. S is the administration manager and is also responsible for legal and compliance functions. H is responsible for customer service and has responsibility for ensuring that customers who have purchased goods from BCD are fully satisfied. Y deals with suppliers and negotiates on the price and quality of inventory. He is also responsible for identifying the most appropriate suppliers of plant and machinery for the factory. P is the information technology manager and is responsible for all information systems within the company.

According to Porter's value chain, which of the managers is involved in a primary activity as opposed to a support activity?

A   S

B   H

C   Y

D   P

40 **As part of a Porter's 5 Forces analysis, which of the following would cause rivalry amongst existing competitors to be higher?**

A   Rapid growth in the market

B   High fixed costs

C   Relative quality and costs of similar products

D   High barriers to entry

41 **Which TWO of the following are the main questions normally addressed by a mission statement?**

A   How will we compete?

B   What are we providing?

C   What is our preferred future?

D   How will we increase our market share?

E   Why do we exist?

42 **The term BRIC refers to which of the following?**

A   Certain national economies

B   Bringing about real continuous improvement

C   A ranking index used in aptitude testing

D   A system for business resource and information capture

43 Political risk analysis is conducted by a company considering international operations and normally focuses on which of the following?

    A   The world economy generally

    B   The relations between the USA, Japan and Europe

    C   The political and cultural differences between the home and target country

    D   The industrialisation of the target country

44 One of the principal insights of the resource-based view of the firm is that not all resources are of equal importance or possess the potential to be a source of sustainable competitive advantage.

What are the four conditions that must be met in order for resources to be advantage-creating?

    A   External, Valuable, Non-substitutable, Differentiated

    B   Valuable, Rare, Imperfectly imitable, Non-substitutable

    C   Expensive, Imperfectly imitable, Intangible, Non-substitutable

    D   Valuable, Imperfectly imitable, Tangible, Rare

45 Bowman's strategy clock suggests eight possible positions for achieving competitive advantage depending on the combination of price, and perceived value to the customer. Four of the positions are shown below, together with descriptions of four approaches. Match the position to the correct description.

Focused differentiation	Companies competing here can build up reputation and customer loyalty for offering reasonable goods at fair prices.
Monopoly pricing	Consumers will be willing to pay high prices in this category as they value the uniqueness and exclusivity of the product.
Low Price	This position can only be achieved where there is only one company in the market or very limited choice for the customer.
Hybrid	Relies on high volumes to counteract the small margins.

46 LMN is a well-established, medium-sized company operating in the travel and tourism industry. LMN is best known for beach resort holidays, but has recently diversified into city breaks. This has been partially successful, and currently comprises approximately 25% of the company's business. Both the beach resort holiday and city break markets are growing steadily. LMN faces strong competition in both of these markets. It currently has a market share of about 15% of the market for beach resort holidays, and around 10% of the market for city-centre holidays.

Which of the following strategic planning techniques is likely to be most appropriate for LMN?

    A   Rational/formal

    B   Emergent

    C   Incrementalism

    D   Freewheeling opportunism

47 Globalisation has increased international trade, but it has also increased risk. Companies can experience country and political risk when they expand their operations into other areas.

Which of the following statements are true in relation to political risk? Select all that apply.

A Political risk is greater in countries with developing economies

B Political risk can be generated by organisations such as the UN

C Political risk is a wider, more general risk than country risk

D Political risk is always direct

E When managing political risk, it is important to take action after the risk has materialised

48 **According to Mintzberg's strategy safari, the approach to strategy development which suggests that 'strategy development is a rational process which seeks to establish a fit between internal capabilities and external possibilities' is known as which of the following?**

A The design school

B The power school

C The learning school

D The configuration school

49 XYZ offers accountancy training courses. The market is growing quickly and XYZ's courses are significantly different to those offered by its rivals. Any new company wishing to teach accountancy courses must obtain accreditation by the various accountancy organisations. This process can take several years.

Based on the above information, which of the following statements can be made about XYZ's competitive environment?

A Competitive rivalry is likely to be low

B Supplier power is likely to be low

C Barriers to entry are likely to be low

D The threat of new entrants is likely to be low

50 **Which TWO of the following statements relating to Big Data are true?**

A Big Data refers to any financial data over $1 billion

B Three of the main defining characteristics of Big Data are Velocity, Volume and Variety

C Managing Big Data effectively can lead to increased competitive advantage

D The term Big Data means 'data that comes from many sources'

E Big Data contains mainly non-financial data

51 ABC is a well-established clothing designer and retailer, catering mainly for the over 60s market. ABC is carrying out a corporate appraisal and some of the findings are shown below. Match these findings to the SWOT heading they would most likely fall under.

- A large cash balance.

- A lack of in-house IT expertise

- A respected and entrepreneurial leader

- Customer resistance to on-line shopping

- Good designs

Strengths	Weaknesses	Opportunities	Threats

52 According to Porter's five forces model, which TWO of the following would tend to indicate there is a low threat of new entrants to the market?

A Low capital requirements

B Patents exist on major product lines

C Access to distribution channels is not restricted

D Existing companies in the market are large

E Rapidly expanding market

53 Cyert and March suggested four techniques for dealing with stakeholder conflict. Which TWO of the following are NOT one of the techniques suggested?

A Satisficing

B Sequential attention

C Weighting and scoring

D Prioritisation

E Exercise of power

54 What are the three levels of strategy seen in an organisation?

A Operational, Business, Tactical

B Corporate, Emergent, Rational

C Corporate, Business, Operational

D Business, Emergent, Operational

55 Country N is home to a large number of internationally successful mobile phone companies. The government of Country N has commissioned a study to determine why this is the case. Which strategic model would be most appropriate to use to answer this question?

A   PESTEL Analysis

B   Porter's Value Chain

C   Porter's 5 Forces

D   Porter's Diamond

56 Considering Porter's value chain analysis, complete the sentences using some of the words provided.

Primary	Procurement	Outbound logistics	Operations
Inbound logistics	Service	Support	Infrastructure

_____ includes distributing the products to customers.

Receiving, storing and handling raw material would come under the heading of _____.

_____ would deal with purchasing of raw materials.

Activities involved in the physical creation of the product or the delivery of the service are known as _____ activities.

57 Which of these points is NOT considered to be a role of competitor analysis according to Wilson and Gilligan?

A   to help management understand their competitive advantages and disadvantages relative to competitors

B   to generate insights into competitors' past, present and potential strategies

C   to give an informed basis for developing future strategies to sustain or establish advantages over competitors

D   to assist with the evaluating the results of strategic investments

58 EFG sells motor vehicles in country V. It has recently discovered that the government is planning a major overhaul of the public transport system in country V, which will significantly increase its speed and comfort, while lowering the cost to make it more attractive.

Under which heading of Porter's five forces model would this issue be included?

A   Barriers to entry

B   Power of suppliers

C   Threat of substitutes

D   Power of buyers

59 **Which of the following strategies should be used to deal with stakeholders who have low power but high interest?**

A   keep informed

B   minimal effort

C   keep satisfied

D   key player

60 **Which of the following are characteristics of emergent strategy? Select all that apply.**

A   Set by senior management (top down)

B   Emerges from repeated patterns of operational behaviour

C   Continuous and evolutionary

D   Carefully planned

E   Enables the organisation to adapt to unforeseen circumstances

THE HUMAN ASPECTS OF THE ORGANISATION

61 **The McKinsey 7S Model has three hard and four soft Ss. Which of the following are the four soft ones?**

    A   Systems, staff, skills and style

    B   Skills, style, structure and systems

    C   Staff, skills, strategy and shared values

    D   Staff, skills, style and shared values

62 **With reference to Johnson and Scholes' cultural web framework, match the correct definitions to the element.**

The daily behaviours and actions of people that signal acceptable behaviour	The paradigm
Who makes the decisions	Rituals and routines
What the organisation is about	Stories and myths
The past events and people talked about inside and outside the company	Power structures

63 **According to Handy, the cultural type which is typified by teamwork, flexibility and commitment is known as what?**

    A   Power culture

    B   Role culture

    C   Task culture

    D   Person culture

64 **Four members of staff in a department came back to work an hour late from lunch:**

Employee 1 has had 2 written warnings about lateness.

Employee 2 has just started work with the company a few days ago.

Employee 3 has already had an informal chat regarding this issue.

Employee 4 has recently returned from a period of suspension for excessive lateness.

What would be the most appropriate next stage of action for each of these employees as part of a disciplinary process?

An oral warning
Dismissal
An informal talk
Disciplinary layoff or suspension

65   Here are four short descriptions of leadership and management theories:

There is one best way to undertake every task.

Interpersonal relations are a key part of determining workplace behaviour.

Managers must control the needs of the task, individual and group.

Managers can be either a psychologically distant or psychologically close.

Match the descriptions above to the correct theory from the following list.

- **Adair's action-centred leadership**

- **Human relations school**

- **McGregor's Theory X and Theory Y**

- **Fiedler's contingency theory**

- **Taylor's scientific management**

- **Blake and Mouton's managerial grid**

66   **In Drucker's Management by Objectives model, he suggests that organisations require multiple objectives. Which of the following are THREE of Drucker's key objectives?**

A   Innovation

B   Public responsibility

C   Employee satisfaction

D   Sales revenue

E   Productivity

F   Market share

67   **Which of the following is NOT an advantage of an effective performance appraisal system?**

A   Improves communication between managers and subordinates

B   Helps identify training needs

C   Ensures performance targets are met

D   Provides a fair process for reward decisions

68   Hofstede developed an influential model of the dimensions on which national cultures differ.

In the Hofstede model, a national culture which is uncomfortable with risk and ambiguity and which would feel threatened by unusual situations would be classified as:

A   individualist

B   masculine

C   low power distance

D   high uncertainty avoidance

69 Handy listed four distinct cultural types:

Power	Role	Task	Person

Match the following statements to the cultural type it relates to.

- A large bureaucratic organisation such as a Government department would likely have this type of culture.

- With this type of culture, everything is based on a logical order and rationality.

- An organisation which is based on the technical expertise of the individual employees would tend to have this type of culture.

- This type of culture would tend to be found in small, owner-run organisations.

70 **Intrinsic satisfaction is said to be derived from which of the following issues?**

A Perks of the job

B Job content

C Job rewards

D Group cohesiveness and belonging

71 **What type of power is a manager using when they promote a member of staff on merit?**

A Referent

B Expert

C Coercive

D Reward

72 **In the Blake and Mouton managerial grid, shown below, match the styles to the correct place on the grid.**

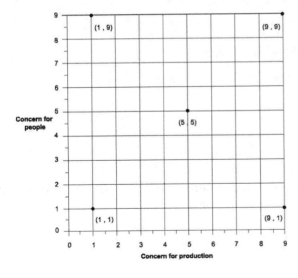

Task orientated
Country-club
Impoverished
Team style
Middle road

73   According to Herzberg's motivation theory, factors can be hygiene factors or motivators. Match the following as to whether they relate to hygiene factors or motivators.

- These help to avoid unpleasantness and dissatisfaction

- Good working conditions

- An appropriate level of salary

- Career advancement

- These satisfy the need for personal growth

74   The final stage in disciplinary action is dismissal. Prior to this stage, a number of other stages should be followed.

1   Oral warning

2   Informal talk

3   Suspension

4   Final written warning

5   First written warning

List the numbers in the order in which the stages would occur in a disciplinary procedure.

A   2, 1, 3, 5, 4

B   1, 5, 2, 4, 3

C   2, 1, 5, 4, 3

D   2, 1, 3, 4, 5

75   Which TWO of the following statements are considered to be advantages of a good grievance procedure?

A   It ensures the legal obligations of the employer are met

B   It improves employee morale and trust

C   It ensures all employees will follow instructions

D   It reduces the number of customer complaints about staff

E   It improves productivity

76 Adair's action-centred leadership model suggests that effective leadership depends on balancing the priority given to three inter-related sets of needs – task, individual and group. Match the following roles to whether they are a task, individual maintenance or group maintenance roles.

Task	Individual maintenance	Group maintenance

- Opinion-seeking
- Feedback
- Peace keeping
- Communicating
- Decision making
- Counselling

77 Within the organisational iceberg, some items are defined as visible and others as hidden. Which of the following would be defined as visible elements? Select all that apply.

A Attitudes

B Goals

C Style

D Values

E Skills

F Technology

78 The following assumptions underlie a well-known theory of motivation.

The expenditure of physical and mental effort at work is as natural as play or rest.

If a job is satisfying, then the result will be commitment to the organisation.

These assumptions apply to which of the following models?

A Maslow's hierarchy of needs

B McGregor's Theory X

C McGregor's Theory Y

D Hertzberg's motivation theory

79 Which approach to control is likely to be found in small owner-managed organisations where there is centralised decision-making by the owner?

A Personal centralised control

B Output control

C Clan or Cultural control

D Bureaucratic control

80   Which of the following statements relating to Health and Safety in the workplace is NOT true?

    A   Managing health and safety in the workplace is a legal requirement

    B   Health and safety controls can save companies money

    C   Managing health and safety is solely the responsibility of directors

    D   Provision of training for employees is part of health and safety requirements

81   Equal opportunities and diversity in the workplace are often confused. Match the following to whether they relate to diversity or equal opportunities?

- Its purpose is to remove discrimination

- It relies on proactive action

- It is a Human Resources role

- It is a managerial role

82   In country A, most businesses are highly bureaucratic with many defined rules for employees. However, even junior staff members are usually involved in the creation of these rules, as they expect to have a say in the running of the business.

Consider the following cultural positions from Hofstede's model of national cultures.

    A   High uncertainty avoidance

    B   Masculinity

    C   Low power distance

    D   Individualism

    E   Long term orientation

Which TWO of the cultural positions identified above are shown to exist in country A?

83   H is a new employee at JHI. O, a long-serving employee, has been asked to offer H any practical advice and support that he needs and act as a role model for H.

O would therefore be classified as H's:

    A   Coach

    B   Mentor

    C   Counsellor

    D   Partner

84 Which of the following statements regarding authority and responsibility are true? Select all that apply.

A   Authority is the right to exercise power.

B   Traditional authority is based on Weber's classical bureaucracy.

C   Responsibility is the capacity to exert influence.

D   When delegating, responsibility can never be delegated.

E   Responsibility means the right to hold subordinates accountable for their performance and achievements.

85 The finance director of CDE, a UK company, is summarily dismissed without notice. His contract of employment gives an entitlement to one year's notice of termination of employment. Under UK law, the director could bring an action for _____ or _____ dismissal.

Which of the following words most accurately fill the gaps?

Redundancy	Termination	Wrongful	Negligence	Unfair

86 ABC, a previously nationalised industry in S Country has recently become privatised as part of a government initiative to encourage competition and innovation. When nationalised, the company held a near monopolistic position but it now faces strong competition from several companies, both from S Country and from other countries.

ABC is finding it very difficult to adapt and they are falling behind competitors in terms of innovation and product development. Departments in ABC find it difficult to work together as they have traditionally focused exclusively on their own specialisms and would be unwilling to do anything outside of their job descriptions.

Which of Handy's cultural types does ABC currently have and which should it move to if it is to successfully compete in its new marketplace?

	Current	New
A	Task	Person
B	Role	Task
C	Person	Task
D	Power	Role

87 **J is a manager with EFG. He does not get on well with the employees who report to him and has little real power to punish or reward the staff for their behaviour. Which of the following management styles does Fiedler suggest would work best for J?**

A   Psychologically close

B   Psychologically open

C   Psychologically committed

D   Psychologically distant

88   Match up the following elements within CDE, an accountancy company, with how they would be classified by Johnson and Scholes' cultural web.

Symbols	There is a timesheet system accounting for each hour of time worked in a week.
Rituals and routines	All decisions on Audit work programmes come from head office.
Control systems	People often work through lunchtime and it's not unusual for people to work after 6pm.
Power structures	There are a finite number of parking spaces allocated to a few key staff members.

89   EFG is a large organisation with a range of incentives available to motivate and improve the performance of its staff. Which of the following incentives will be most appropriate for staff working in the HR department?

   A   Commission

   B   Piece rate

   C   Profit sharing

   D   Productivity plans

90   A manager is planning on introducing a new computer system into her department. She plans to offer her staff bonuses to encourage them to use the new system, as well as relying on her own personal charisma.

   Which TWO of the following sources of power is the manager planning to use?

   A   Reward

   B   Legitimate

   C   Referent

   D   Coercive

   E   Expert

91   The Equality Act 2012 aims to strengthen the protection against discrimination in the workplace and in the wider society. According to the act, it is unlawful to discriminate against people on a number of grounds. Which of the following grounds for discrimination is NOT covered by the act?

   A   Marriage and civil partnership

   B   Religion or belief

   C   Physical appearance

   D   Age

92 **Which of the following is NOT a requirement of effective delegation?**

   A   Clearly defining the subordinate's goals and the limits of the delegated authority

   B   Ensuring that the subordinate will be able to undertake the task competently

   C   Backing off so that the subordinate has to perform the task unassisted

   D   Reviewing results and offering feedback on performance at agreed points

93 **Which TWO of the following would be a justified reason for redundancy?**

   A   Where an employee's conduct is unacceptable

   B   Where a department or team persistently underperforms

   C   Where an employee is no longer legally able to perform the role

   D   Where the type of work which the employee undertakes is no longer carried out

   E   Where an employee's part of the business ceases trading

94 **In a typical hierarchical organisation, the requirement of a lower-level manager to answer to a higher-level manager in the chain of command is referred to as:**

   A   authority

   B   empowerment

   C   accountability

   D   super-ordination

95 **At which level of control within an organisation would the setting of the control environment be a responsibility?**

   A   Strategic

   B   Operational

   C   Tactical

   D   Group

96 **According to Schein, culture exist at three levels: 'Artefacts', 'Values' and 'Basic assumptions'. Which TWO of the following relate to Values?**

   A   The things that can be seen, heard and observed

   B   Deeply held beliefs

   C   The things that can be identified from stories

   D   The way we do things around here

   E   How people justify what they do

97 **Which of the following is seen as a DISADVANTAGE of having a strong culture?**

    A   Strong cultures may regulate behaviour and norms within the organisation

    B   Strong cultures may reduce differences amongst the members of the organisation

    C   Strong cultures may affect the organisation's ability or desire to learn new skills

    D   Strong cultures may facilitate good communication and coordination within the organisation

98 **Which three of the following are management functions identified by Fayol?**

    A   Co-ordinating

    B   Controlling

    C   Communicating

    D   Delegating

    E   Motivating

    F   Organising

99 **Which THREE of the following statements regarding management concepts are correct?**

    A   Responsibility can be delegated but authority cannot

    B   Authority can be delegated but responsibility cannot

    C   The scope of responsibility must always exceed the scope of authority

    D   Traditional authority is based on custom and practice

    E   Power is the ability to exert influence

    F   Delegation is where employees are given autonomy and responsibility to undertake tasks without being directed at each step by management.

100 **In the context of a balanced scorecard approach to the provision of management information, which TWO of the following measures might be appropriate for monitoring the innovation and learning perspective?**

    A   Training days per employee

    B   Employee satisfaction

    C   Cost income ratio

    D   Percentage of revenue generated by new products and services

    E   Customer satisfaction

MANAGING RELATIONSHIPS

101 G is a member of a project team. His colleagues in the team rely on him to read and check complex project documentation. G has a keen eye for detail and often identifies minor details in documents that others miss but may be of significance. Despite this diligent approach, G always meets his deadlines. However, Some of G's colleagues feel frustrated when he refuses to involve others. He can hold up progress as he will not agree to the team signing off project documents until all of his concerns are fully discussed.

According to Belbin's team roles theory, G is an example of which of the following?

A   Implementer

B   Completer-finisher

C   Monitor-evaluator

D   Shaper

102   **Match the types of conflict to the correct statement:**

Horizontal	Tends to cause alienation between groups and individuals
Vertical	Considered positive and beneficial to the organisation
Constructive	Occurs between departments at the same level in the organisation
Destructive	Occurs between individuals and groups at different levels

103   J manages a team of workers within her department. She has recently sat in on a team meeting during which the team had started discussing which roles each team member would take on.

Which of Tuckman's stages of group development does J's team appear to have reached?

A   Storming

B   Norming

C   Performing

D   Forming

104   **According to transaction cost theory, the mechanisms that organisations have to choose between to control their resources and carry out their operations are:**

A   markets or structures

B   hierarchies or markets

C   structures or culture

D   hierarchies or culture

105 Belbin suggested a number of team roles including the following:

Team worker	Plant	Monitor-Evaluator	Completer Finisher	Implementer (company worker)

Match the following personalities to the appropriate role defined by Belbin.

A S is a very quiet person, she often reserves her opinion until being directly asked for it however she always offers unusual and creative suggestions when the team is faced with difficult problem

B J is respected by all team members for his analytical skills, though he rarely gets invited to out-of-office private parties as many find him tactless

C E is the company's HR manager, she ensures that any potential conflicts are promptly identified and resolved and the team members work harmoniously

106 Which of the following LEAST accurately completes the statement: 'A win-win negotiation strategy is most likely when...'

A both parties are aggressive

B both parties focus on problem-solving strategies

C both parties adopt a collaborative approach

D both parties are assertive

107 EFG has a large marketing department. In which THREE of the following ways would this department co-ordinate with EFG's finance department?

A Decisions on the quantity of raw materials required

B Establishing credit terms for customers

C Budgeting for sales volumes

D Calculating pay rises for staff

E Decisions on the selling price of the product

F Determining market share

108 Which of the following statements is/are correct with regards to the differences between individuals and teams? Select all that apply.

A Teams tend to enjoy synergies which cannot be achieved by individual workers

B Teams tend to make decisions more rapidly than individuals

C Individuals are less likely to make definite decisions and rely on compromises

D There are fewer controls in place when groups make decisions

E Teams tend to make more risky, or more cautious, decisions than individuals.

109   There are a number of techniques which can be used to manage inter-group conflict, including:

Third party consultants	Member rotation	Superordinate goals	Confrontation

Match the following descriptions to the correct technique.

- This technique involves the conflicting party directly engaging with each other and negotiating with one another to try to work out their differences.

- This technique involves management imposing shared targets on both parties which will require the cooperation of both parties in order to meet the target.

- With this technique, members of one department will be asked to work in the other department for a period of time, to allow them to better understand the issues faced by the other department.

- A technique which can be used where conflicting parties are uncooperative is to bring in an independent party to meet with the conflicting parties to encourage them to reach agreement.

110   **Which of the following can be used to describe the homogeneity of objectives and thinking in group work?**

A   The Abilene Paradox

B   Risky shift

C   Group polarisation

D   Groupthink

111   **The four steps to negotiating an agreement go in what order:**

A   persuade other party, know the background, influence the other party, agreement is reached

B   proposing a solution, clarifying objectives, narrow the gap, obtain feedback

C   information gathering, present their starting positions, narrow the gap, agreement is reached

D   information gathering, present their starting positions, look for a mutually beneficial outcome, narrow the gap

112   Mainwaring suggested four conflict managing strategies:

stimulation and orchestration	suppression	reduction	resolution

Match the strategy to the definitions given below:

A   involves the use or threatened use of authority or force

B   seeks to eliminate the root causes of conflict

C   involves building on areas of agreement and on common objectives

D   actively encourages conflict as a means of generating new ideas and new approaches or of stimulating change

113 According to Cialdini, when trying to influence another person, the following six principles of influence can be used:

- Reciprocity

- Commitment

- Social proof

- Liking

- Authority

- Scarcity

Match the following actions taken to the correct principle.

A   Remind the person of things you have done for them in the past

B   Advise people that they could lose out if they don't act quickly

C   Use the opinions of those already supporting you to influence others to join that support

D   Building relationships with the people you want to influence so that they trust you.

114 **Match the definitions to the correct type of asset specificity.**

The assets may be immobile or attached to a particular location	Dedicated asset
The unique ability to provide a service at a certain time	Physical asset
An asset with unique properties	Site
An asset made to an exact specification and has only one application	Temporal

115 **Research on group effectiveness has concluded that the most consistently successful groups:**

A   are those in which all members are innovative

B   comprise a range of roles undertaken by various members

C   are those in which all members are very intelligent

D   comprise a range of roles all undertaken by a few members of the group

116 Tuckman identified five stages in group development.

In which order do the stages occur?

A   Forming, adjourning, storming, performing, norming

B   Forming, norming, storming, performing, adjourning

C   Storming, forming, performing, adjourning, norming

D   Forming, storming, norming, performing, adjourning

117 The finance function can be positioned in different ways within the organisation.

Complete the following sentences relating the positioning of finance using some of the following words.

Consistency	Reduced	Increased
Business partnering	Business Process Outsourcing	Shared services centres

When the finance function is carried out by an external party, this is known as _____.

With _____ the confidentiality risk is _____.

_____ premises costs and _____ quality of service provision are benefits of _____.

With _____ the knowledge of the business area is _____ but there can be duplication of effort across the organisation.

118 **The conflict management strategy recommended by the Thomas-Kilmann Conflict Mode Instrument as a means of finding a win:win situation is which of the following?**

A   compromising

B   competing

C   collaborating

D   accommodating

119 **Which of the following statements about non-verbal communication is NOT true?**

A   Non-verbal actions can vary across countries and cultures

B   The actual words said are just as important as the way they are said

C   Physical gestures such as a hand shake or a pat on the back are considered non-verbal communication

D   Appearance and posture are important elements of communication

120 **Negotiation is a process in which:**

A   two or more parties try to initiate differences

B   two or more parties try to avoid differences

C   two or more parties try to prevent differences

D   two or more parties try to resolve differences

121 **Match the different team roles, as defined by Belbin, to the following descriptions:**

Plant	Supports other members of the team and helps to promote harmony.
Completer Finisher	Imaginative and very good at coming up with original ideas and suggestions.
Team Worker	Gives attention to detail and is concerned with meeting deadlines.

122 Which TWO of the following are strategies for managing conflict explained by Mainwaring?

A   suppression

B   negotiation

C   discipline

D   reduction

E   persuasion

123 Tuckman's team development model explains that, as a team develops and relationships become more established, the leadership style should change.

What name did Tuckman give to the stage of team development in which the team responds well to the team leader, roles and responsibilities are clear and accepted, commitment is strong and major decisions are taken by group agreement?

A   Storming

B   Performing

C   Forming

D   Norming

124 Which of the following are all types of asset specificity?

A   brand name, dedicated, cost, style

B   human asset, site, temporal, flexible

C   dedicated, physical, temporal, brand name

D   intangible, human asset, brand name, site

125 In Belbin's team roles, which role is defined as 'committed to the task, may be aggressive and challenging, will always promote activity'?

A   Shaper

B   Plant

C   Team Worker

D   Completer Finisher

126 Identify, in the correct order, the four main stages in the negotiation process.

1	Bargaining
2	Preparation
3	Closing
4	Opening

127 **Vaill suggested that high performing teams had a number of common characteristics. Which TWO of the following are some of those characteristics?**

   A   Strong and clear leadership

   B   The team should be of limited duration

   C   The team should be small

   D   Generation of inventions and new methods

   E   Voluntary membership

128 **Which of the following statements regarding Finance's relationship with professional advisors is NOT true?**

   A   It is important to be open with advisors to let them get to know your business.

   B   It is important to maintain good relationships with professional advisors in case they are needed at short notice.

   C   Advisors would only be contacted when sales or profits are low.

   D   Examples of professional advisors used by organisations are solicitors, tax consultants and environmental advisors.

129 **Group working can bring many advantages, but it can also bring some problems. Match the problem with group working with its description.**

Conformity	Groups can end up taking decisions which are riskier than the individual members would take
Abilene paradox	Group members reach consensus without critically testing, analysing and evaluating ideas
Risky shift	The group can end up with an outcome which none of the members wanted
Groupthink	Individuals within the group can be persuaded to accept decisions which they know to be wrong

130 **When working in groups, the combined activity of the group can be greater than the sum of the activities of each member of the group. What is the name given to this phenomenon?**

   A   Norming

   B   Groupthink

   C   Synergy

   D   Conformity

131 Mainwaring suggested a number of causes of conflict including:

Interdependencies
Misunderstandings
Conviction beliefs
History

Complete the following sentences using some of the above words:

Where boundaries between departments are not clearly defined, this can cause problems of _____.

Communication problems can lead to _____.

_____ suggests that conflict tends to be self-perpetuating.

132 **Match the element of the communication process to its description.**

What is being transmitted	Decoding
The medium through which the message is being sent	Feedback
The message is translated and its meaning is generated	Channel
The receiver responds to the message	Noise
Anything which stops the message being transmitted as intended	Message

133 There are two types of conflict within an organisation:

Horizontal		Vertical

Match the following statements to whether they relate to horizontal or vertical conflict.

A   Conflict occurring between groups and departments at the same level in the hierarchy.

B   Where functional specialisms cause differences in cognitive and emotional orientations.

C   A reward system based only departmental performance may encourage managers to meet goals at the expenses of other departments.

D   Physiological distance can make workers feel isolated from the organisation.

134 According to Cialdini, there are six principles of influence:

Reciprocity
Commitment
Social Proof
Liking
Authority
Scarcity

Match the following descriptions to the correct principle.

A   Identify what you want to achieve and what you need from the other person then consider what you may be able to offer them

B   Build relationships with those you want to influence so that they trust you

C   Use the opinions of those already supporting you to influence others to join that support

135 **Which of the following statements relating to non-verbal communication is NOT true?**

A   Maintaining eye contact is an important element of non-verbal communication

B   Non-verbal actions can help to ensure that the message is communicated correctly

C   Non-verbal actions are universally understood

D   The tone used when conversing is an important part of the communication process

136 The finance function can be positioned in three main ways:

Business partnering	Shared services centre (SSC)	Business process outsourcing (BPO)

Match the following definitions to the correct position above.

A   The finance function is carried out by an external party

B   A dedicated finance function is set up within each business unit

C   The finance function is consolidated and run as a central unit within the organisation

137 **Match the problems with meetings with the actions which could be taken to avoid them.**

Attendees talk too much	Ensure the correct attendees are invited
Objectives of the meeting are unclear	Ensure action points agreed and minutes of meeting are issued
Action points from previous meetings not carried out	Agenda should be circulated before the meeting
Lack of enthusiasm at the meeting	Chairperson should impose order

138   **Which of the following statements about persuasion are true?**

  A   Persuasion is a weaker form of influence

  B   Persuasion can be direct or indirect

  C   The six principles of influence can be used in persuasion

  D   In persuasion you are basically telling the other person what to do

139   The finance function can be carried out within the business unit (business partner), by a third party (BPO) or internally in a shared service centre (SSC).

  Which of the following comments relating to BPO are true?

  A   Using BPO will often lead to the loss of best practice

  B   BPO will offer more control over information provided

  C   Using BPO will result in losing economies of scale

  D   A risk of BPO is the loss of intellectual property

140   **The strategy for managing conflict which involves building on areas of agreement and on common objectives, and changing attitudes and perceptions of the parties involved is known as which of the following?**

  A   Conflict stimulation and orchestration

  B   Conflict suppression

  C   Conflict reduction

  D   Conflict resolution

MANAGING CHANGE THROUGH PROJECTS

141   **Which of the following would be an internal trigger for change in an organisation?**

   A   A major acquisition

   B   Changes in fashion trends

   C   New legislation for protection of the environment

   D   Trade union demands for a shorter working week for all employees

142   A number of tools are used in planning for activities and costs within a project, including:

Work breakdown structure
Work packages and Statements of work
Product breakdown structure
Cost breakdown structure

   Match the tool to its purpose from the following list.

To specify the work to be done for each activity and who will carry it out
To cost each element of the project
To divide the work to be carried out into manageable pieces
To identify the product purchases required for each activity

143   **Configuration management is designed to:**

   A   track deviation from proposed deliverables

   B   track deviation from schedule

   C   track product changes and versions

   D   track co-ordination between different project teams

144   **According to Gido and Clements, during which phase in the project lifecycle would a feasibility study be undertaken?**

   A   Identification of a need

   B   Development of a proposed solution

   C   Implementation

   D   Completion

145   Lewin's force field analysis model in organisation identifies driving forces and restraining forces that influence change.

When there is strong resistance to change, Lewin recommended that the most effective way for management to achieve the desired change would be to do which of the following? Select all that apply.

A   increase the strength of the driving forces

B   reduce the strength of the driving forces

C   increase the strength of the restraining forces

D   reduce the strength of the restraining forces

146   **Match the benefit to the project management tool.**

Resource histogram	Establishes the authority and responsibility for each part of the project
Critical path analysis	Identifies the activities that cannot overrun without delaying the overall project completion
PERT	Allows a calculation of contingency to be added to the project plan
Breakdown structures	Helps with capacity planning

147   **Why does Lewin refer to the first stage of his three-stage change model as unfreezing?**

A   Because there is a need to melt existing patterns of behaviour

B   Because of the impact of global warming on corporate activity

C   Because employees are showing resistance to the proposed change

D   Because the company is lagging behind its competitors in terms of innovation

148   **Kanter argued that change-adept organisations (organisations that manage change successfully) share three key attributes. Which of the following are these three attributes?**

A   imagination to innovate, openness to collaborate, professionalism to perform

B   openness to collaborate, professionalism to perform, resilience to survive

C   professionalism to perform, imagination to innovate, resilience to survive

D   resilience to survive, openness to collaborate, imagination to innovate

149   In the PRINCE2 project organisational structure, a team that provides an independent view of how the project is progressing, reflecting business, user and specialist interests, is called a project _____ team.

Which of the following words correctly fills the gap in the above definition?

A   Steering

B   Management

C   Assurance

D   Support

150 The Project Management Institute's five process areas are:

A   Executing

B   Initiating

C   Closing

D   Controlling

E   Planning

Place the process area in the correct place in the following diagram:

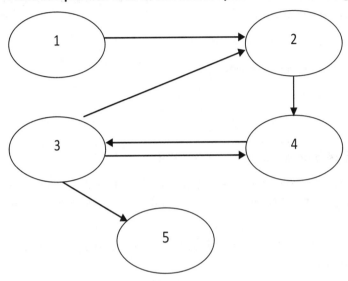

151 **Who is ultimately responsible for closing down an unsuccessful project?**

A   Project team

B   Project steering committee

C   Project owner

D   Project customer

152 **A hierarchical view of the way a project is structured, identifying progressively detailed task elements, is known as which of the following?**

A   CBS

B   CPA

C   WBS

D   PID

153 **Within a business strategy a change that is to be implemented quickly and will be radical is known as?**

A   Adaptation

B   Evolution

C   Reconstruction

D   Revolution

154 The extent of work needed to produce the project's deliverables is known as which of the following?

    A   scale

    B   cycle

    C   time frame

    D   scope

155 A project manager requires a number of skills. Which of the following is not a skill not necessarily required by a project manager?

    A   leadership and delegation

    B   change management and problem-solving

    C   specialist financial

    D   negotiation

Questions 156, 157 and 158 are based on the following scenario:

C is in charge of a group of 15 people involved in a series of complex projects in the same field. The group has been working together amicably and successfully for a considerable time. Its members value C's leadership.

The next project that the group is expected to carry out has the following activities, time estimates (in months) and precedences:

Activity	Precedence	Duration
A	–	4
B	–	3
C	A	6
D	B	8
E	C, D	3

156 In the scenario, the team's stage of development in terms of Tuckman is:

    A   Forming

    B   Storming

    C   Norming

    D   Performing

157 In the scenario, calculate the overall duration of the next project.

    _____months

158   In the scenario, for the next project, the critical path is:

   A   A C E

   B   B D E

   C   A B D E

   D   A B C D E

159   Beer and Nohria identified two approaches to transformational change within an organisation, the Theory E and Theory O approaches. Theory E is a 'hard' approach based on maximising economic value and Theory O is a 'soft' approach based on organisational capability.

   According to Beer and Nohria, when the management of an organisation wish to implement transformational change, which of the following would be the most effective approach?

   A   Theory O approach only

   B   Theory E approach first, followed by the Theory O approach

   C   Theory O approach first, followed by the Theory E approach

   D   Theory E and Theory O approaches simultaneously

160   **Among project stakeholders, the person/group that is the source of the project manager's authority, and acts as agent of the organisation to ensure that the project achieves its objectives is called:**

   A   The project owner

   B   The project customer

   C   The project champion

   D   The project sponsor

161   **Which of the following is an example of incremental change within an organisation?**

   A   Downsizing

   B   Introducing a new IT system

   C   Restructuring

   D   Changing the corporate culture

162   **Which of the following planning techniques takes the form of a component (or 'stacked') vertical bar chart?**

   A   Gantt chart

   B   Resource histogram

   C   Network diagram

   D   Work breakdown structure

163 Which tool or technique, which is used for planning the time of a project, is used to measure how far the project has progressed and how far it has to run?

A   Gate

B   Milestone

C   Critical path

D   PERT

164 Which type of feasibility investigates whether project requirements can be met using available material, technology and processes?

A   Economic

B   Social

C   Ecological

D   Technical

165 Which of the following are key areas of the Project Management Body of Knowledge (PMBOK)? Select all that apply

A   Integration

B   Procurement

C   Feasibility

D   Human resources

E   Planning

F   Control

166 Which of the following statements about the matrix organisation structure is true?

A   It can improve lateral communication and cooperation between specialists

B   It can enhance reporting between subordinates and managers

C   It can minimise time spent in meetings

D   It is most useful where for companies with multiple projects where all the projects are running at the same time

167 Which of the following is NOT one of the PRINCE2 process areas?

A   Managing stage boundaries

B   Managing product delivery

C   Risk management

D   Controlling

168   **Which of the following project stakeholders is the person who provides the resources for the project?**

    A   Project sponsor

    B   Project manager

    C   Project owner

    D   Project customer

169   **Identify roles A, B, C and D missing from the basic PRINCE2 project organisational structure from the options below.**

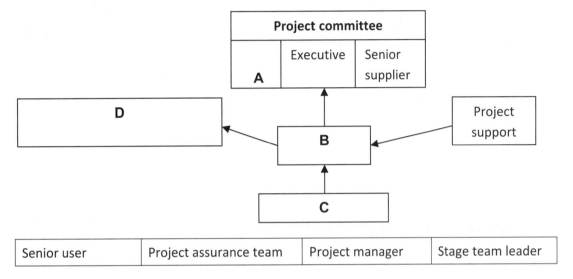

Senior user	Project assurance team	Project manager	Stage team leader

170   **A final report is produced at the end of the project. Which of the following would NOT be included in the final report?**

    A   Actual achievement in relation to costs and project schedules

    B   Customer's original requirement and original project deliverable

    C   The extent to which the benefits defined in the original business case have been achieved

    D   List of deliverables which the customer received

171   The management of a hospital is trying to persuade its doctors and qualified medical staff that due to a chronic shortage of trained medical staff throughout the country, the problems that the hospital faces in dealing with patients will be eased if unqualified staff are given training to carry out certain types of medical treatment on patients.

    According to Lewin's three-step model of change, which stage in the process is gaining acceptance by qualified staff of the need to allow unqualified staff to treat patients?

    A   Unfreezing

    B   Movement

    C   Re-freezing

    D   Cooling

172 **Which of the following factors is most likely to lead to successful organisational change?**

    A   Imposed by external consultants

    B   Maintaining existing policies and procedures

    C   Autocratic leadership

    D   Initiated and supported by top management

173 Consider the following network diagram of a simple project.

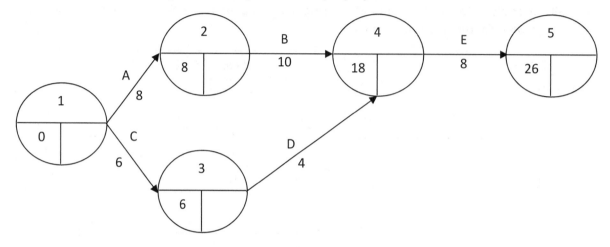

Calculate the float time on activity C.

_____ **days**

174 **At what stage in the project life cycle is the scope of a project determined?**

    A   Planning

    B   Initiating

    C   Executing

    D   Controlling

175 **Planned organisational change is most commonly triggered by the need to respond to new threats or opportunities presented by which of the following?**

    A   the organisation's culture

    B   developments in the external environment

    C   the internal environment

    D   action by the organisation's management

176 A change that aims to allow the business to maintain its current market share by adopting minor initiatives over the next few years would be known as _____.

A change that is implemented gradually through inter-related initiatives is known as _____.

Complete the above sentences by using some of the following words.

- Adaptation
- Evolution
- Reconstruction
- Revolution

177 **Which of the following would NOT generally be part of configuration management within a project?**

A   Authorisation and tracking of changes

B   Version control for documentation

C   Access control over project records

D   Progress reporting

178 **In a project, when there are conflicting objectives, a strategy to please 'as many of the stakeholders as much of the time as possible' is known as:**

A   Sequential attention

B   Satisficing

C   Optimising

D   Prioritising

179 A key skill required by a project manager is leadership. Blake & Mouton's managerial grid assesses leadership styles along two axes – concern for task performance and concern for people/relationships.

Each of these is graded on a scale of 1 to 9. Which managerial style did they describe as 'team management'?

A   Very high concern for people and very low concern for the task

B   Very high concern for the task and very low concern for people

C   Very high concern for people and very high concern for the task

D   Very low concern for people and very low concern for the task

180   Based on the principles of 'one person – one boss' and a decision-making authority, Gido
       and Clements's project hierarchy is shown below.

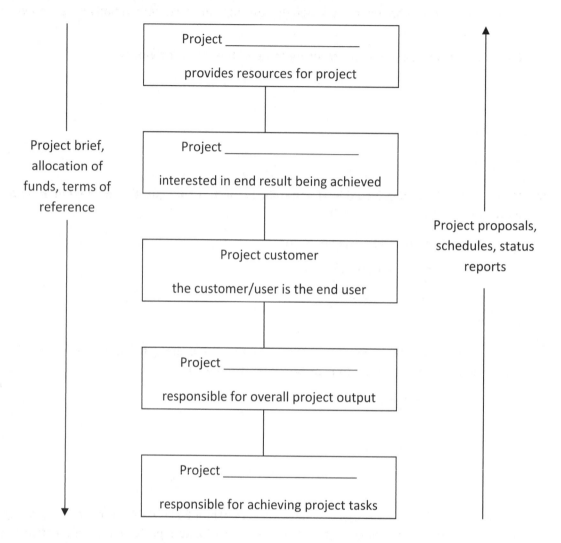

Complete the diagram by inserting the correct stakeholder from the following options:

owner	manager	sponsor	user	team	champion

181   Which of the following activities would NOT be carried out as part of the executing stage
       of an information systems project?

A   Software testing

B   Preparation of training materials

C   Installation and changeover procedures

D   Carrying out a risk analysis

182 Match the following descriptions to the types of change being described.

Evolution	Reconstruction	Adaptation	Revolution

- A change that is to be implemented over a long period of time but will radically alter the business operations.

- A change to realign the way in which the organisation operates, implemented in a series of small steps.

- A change to realign the way in which the organisation operates, with many initiatives being implemented simultaneously.

- Transformational change that occurs via simultaneous initiatives on many fronts.

183 Teams are formed to undertake projects. As teams are developing, they go through a number of stages. At which stage of group formation and development does establishing standards and agreeing ways of working occur?

A   Storming

B   Performing

C   Norming

D   Forming

184 Which of the following statements regarding Gantt charts is/are NOT correct? Select all that apply.

A   A Gantt chart can show planned and actual activity durations on the same chart

B   A Gantt chart is an alternative or complementary approach to network analysis

C   Gantt charts can be used in both planning and control of a project

D   A Gantt chart is a stacked, vertical bar chart

E   A Gantt chart is drawn in real time

185 Which of the following would be items focused on by a conformance management system?

A   Prioritising change requests, recording of changes and agreement of a change budget

B   Functional quality and client satisfaction measures

C   Inspection, quality control and quality assurance

D   Access control over project records and version control for documentation

186 Which three of the following are used as a control element within projects?

A   Project reports

B   Exception reports

C   Project meetings

D   Feasibility study

E   Scenario planning

187 Which of these techniques would be used at the completion stage of a project?

    A   Progress reports

    B   Gantt chart

    C   External review

    D   PERT

188 Which of these meetings would take place regularly with the objective of providing an update on the status of the project?

    A   Team meetings

    B   Progress review meetings

    C   Problem solving meetings

    D   Business review meeting

189 Which ONE of the following is a part of the 'identification of need' phase of the project life cycle?

    A   The Completion Report

    B   The Milestone Review

    C   Project scheduling

    D   The Project Initiation Document

Questions 190 and 191 are based on the following diagram. Durations are shown in weeks.

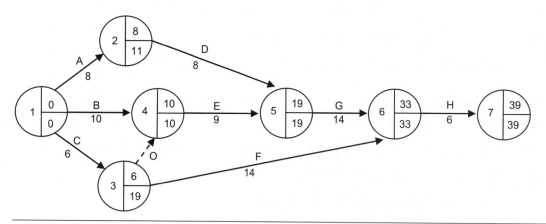

190 Identify the critical path.

    A   ADGH

    B   CFH

    C   BEGH

    D   CEGH

191 **Which of the following statements regarding the diagram are true? Select all that apply.**

A The slack on activities C and F is 14 weeks

B If activity E was to overrun, the project duration would increase.

C Activity D could take 3 weeks longer and the project would still be completed on time.

D Activities A, C and D can start straight away.

E If activity H took 10 weeks, the overall duration of the project would be 43 weeks.

192 **It is important to identify risks within projects and to consider how these risks can be managed. Where a risk is identified as having high likelihood but low impact, the most appropriate risk management approach would be:**

A Transfer

B Avoid

C Reduce

D Accept

193 **When planning for time within a project, account must be taken of risk and uncertainty and there are a number of techniques which can assist with this. Which of the following techniques involves adding artificial slack into risky activities?**

A Scenario planning

B Buffering

C Float

D PERT

194 **Project managers may have to adapt their management style as the project progresses. A management approach that focuses on adapting management behaviour to the particular circumstances of the organisation and to each given situation is known as:**

A Participative leadership

B Scientific management

C Laissez-faire

D Contingency theory

195 **One role of project managers is to motivate the project team. If the project manager adopted Douglas McGregor's Theory X approach, what would they believe people are motivated by? Select all that apply.**

A money and security

B achievement at work

C interpersonal relationships

D recognition for good work

E increased responsibility

196   Which of the following statements about project management software are true? Select all that apply.

A   Software can provide a central store for project documentation

B   Using software will ensure the project delivers within budget

C   The software makes it easier to produce diagrams such as Gantt charts

D   Project management software is generally expensive and complex

E   The software could include central calendars for managing meetings during the project

197   A worry that changes within the organisation will make the work more monotonous would come under which heading for resistance to change?

A   Social factors

B   Personal factors

C   Job factors

D   Economic factors

198   Which three of the following statements regarding the matrix structure are correct?

A   The matrix structure combines the benefits of decentralisation and co-ordination

B   Within the matrix structure, employees will have dual reporting lines

C   The matrix structure is largely theoretical and is rarely used in practice

D   The matrix structure is especially useful when an organisation is undertaking a single large project affecting the whole organisation

E   The matrix structure should lead to less duplication across projects and therefore save money

199   Which TWO of the following are approaches to managing resistance to change as defined by Kotter and Schlesinger?

A   Participation

B   Persuasion

C   Suppression

D   Facilitation and support

E   Delegation

200   According to Herzberg's theory of motivation, which of the following should be in place to avoid dissatisfaction? Select all that apply.

A   Team working

B   Career enhancement

C   Pleasant physical and working conditions

D   Appropriate level of salary and status for the job

E   Increasing levels of responsibility

Section 2

ANSWERS TO OBJECTIVE TEST QUESTIONS

STRATEGIC MANAGEMENT AND THE GLOBAL ENVIRONMENT

1   **A, C and D**

Drucker's other two fundamental questions are:

Who is our customer? and

What are our results?

2   **D**

The definition of critical success factors is 'Those things which must go right if the objectives and goals of an organisation are to be achieved'.

3   **A, D and E**

The fourth method suggested by Cyert and March was exercise of power.

4   **Social**

The social aspect of PESTLE analysis will consider such things as population shifts, age profiles, attitudes, values and beliefs. Cultural or demographic factors would generally be considered under this heading.

5   **The full diagram for the rational (formal) model is shown below.**

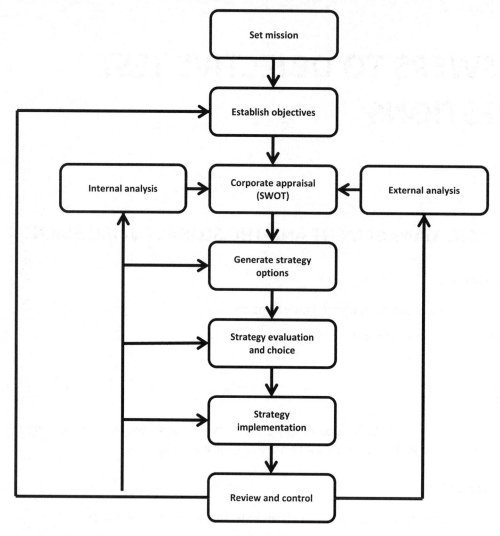

6   **C**

The relatively low cost of the machine and licence, together with the fact that an unskilled person would only require a two day training course suggests that it would fairly easy for anyone to enter the market. Using the five forces model would conclude that the threat of new entrants is high.

No information is given in the question regarding the powers of the buyers or suppliers or the rivalry within the industry.

7 **The completed diagram for Ansoff's matrix is shown below.**

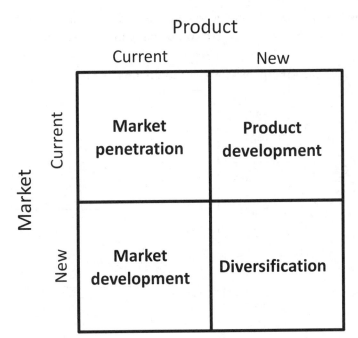

Product

8 The force which would consider this information is **Rivalry** and from the scenario, the force would be **High.**

The threat from rivals will be high as the four main players are similar size and account for the majority of the market. The leading company holds 26% of the market. In addition, the market is growing slowly therefore to make inroads into this market it will require to take some market share from one of the main players which they would resist strongly.

9 **C**

Where a potential problem is viewed as insignificant and short-term, it is likely that the organisation will do nothing.

10 The employees would have high interest and low power therefore the correct strategy for managing them would be **keep informed.**

11   A and C

Globalisation has made it easier for companies to compete anywhere in the world. Options B, D and E would tend to restrict how and where companies can operate.

12   The completed diagram for the emergent strategy should look like this:

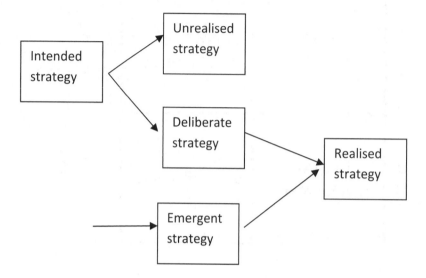

13   B

Factor conditions are those endowments that a country has available and would include the availability of raw materials, suitable infrastructure and a supply of suitably trained labour. Factor conditions are largely natural and not created as a matter of policy or strategy.

14   Qualitative research involves the collection of non-numerical data. It investigates the WHY decisions that consumers make. **Quantitative** research involves gathering factual and numerical data which can then be analysed using **trend** analysis or **ratios**.

15   B

If the maturity stage of the product lifecycle is reached quickly, the firm is more likely to enter the export market sooner, therefore if products are slow to reach maturity they will continue to operate in the home market for longer and the home demand conditions will be enhanced.

16   C

Numerous suppliers would suggest that supplier power is low and in terms of barriers to entry, if anything this would enhance the likelihood of entering the market.

17   **The correct definitions are:**

Strategies which can arise as a result of developing a strategy but changing it in light of new and better opportunities.	Emergent strategy
Strategies which involve taking small steps towards the desired outcome.	Incremental strategy
Strategies which are forced on the organisation by circumstances	Imposed strategy

18   **B**

Stakeholders with low interest and high power can easily increase their level of interest which would make them key to any decisions being made. The best way to manage such stakeholders is to keep them satisfied in order to keep them from moving from quadrant III to quadrant IV.

19   **The correct matching is shown below:**

Its staff are expert in their industry and no other company has the level of knowledge and experience that BCD has - **Resource audit**

The key raw material required for its product is only available from one main supplier - **Porter's five forces**

Customers value the high level of after sales care they receive from BCD - **Porter's value chain**

The government of the country where BCD operates is planning to introduce a tax on the type of products which BCD manufactures - **PESTLE**

20   **D**

Porter identified five primary activities: Inbound logistics, Operations, Outbound logistics, Marketing and sales and Service. Service includes all the activities which occur after the point of sale.

Procurement, Technology development and Human resources management are all support activities.

21   **A, B and D**

Barriers to entry to a market are those aspects which make it difficult for a new company to enter the market. Potential entrants to the market will want the barriers to be low, but existing companies operating in the market will want the barriers to be high to stop new entrants coming in to the market and intensifying competition.

22   B

The business level strategy sits between the corporate level and the operational level and is concerned with how a division or business unit approaches a particular market. At the strategic level the industry in which the business operates will be decided. At the business level, decisions will be based around how they should compete within that chosen industry.

23   The correct definitions are shown below:

Market share	The portion of a market controlled by a particular company or product.
Market size	The number of individuals in a certain market who are potential buyers and/or sellers of a product or service.
Market growth	The increase in the demand for a particular product or service over time.

24   C

Corporate appraisal is also known as SWOT analysis which is used to identify strengths, weaknesses, opportunities and threats.

25   A and C

The rational/formal planning approach to strategy facilitates control and coordination according to a plan, resulting in the whole organisation working towards the same goals (goal congruence). The predefined plan of action and the clearly set targets enable the success of the strategy to be reviewed. However, the process is relatively time-consuming, making response to change slow, and the environmental analysis involved is relatively expensive. This makes it less useful in smaller organisations and organisations operating in dynamic environments.

26   The correct matching is:

Corporate level	• Decisions about acquisitions, mergers and sell-offs
	• Decisions about how integrated the business should be
Business level	• Decisions about what products should be developed
	• Decisions about how to gain competitive advantage
Functional level	• Decisions about how to run the business on a day-to-day basis

27   D

The resource-based view is often known as the inside-out view and sees competitive advantage as coming from the unique assets or core competences possessed by the organisation. These are the things which an organisation has or can do that other companies find difficult to copy.

28   A and E

Objectives should be SMART:

Specific (a specific target)

Measurable

Achievable

Relevant (to aims or goals)

Time bound

29   C

Market penetration is when an organisation seeks to maintain or increase its share of existing markets with existing products. Product development involves developing new products to sell within its existing markets, while market development involves sells existing products in new markets. Diversification is the hardest strategy to implement as it involves developing new products and new markets.

30   The correct matching of the definitions is shown below:

The age at which people are allowed to drink alcohol	Legal
Government tax on sales of alcohol	Political
The level of disposable income people have	Economic
People's religious beliefs and attitudes towards alcohol	Social

31   A

The three Es in a not-for-profit organisation are:

Effectiveness (outputs)

Efficiency (the link between outputs and inputs)

Economy (inputs)

32   A

According to Porter, organisations can generate competitive advantage through:

- cost leadership (offering the same quality as competitors but at a lower price)
- differentiation (offering innovative and high quality products which can be differentiated from rival products and for which high prices can be gained)
- focus (concentrating on a small, niche part of the market).

33   B

SMART stands for Specific, Measurable, Achievable, Relevant and Timely.

34   B and E

Presence of skilled fashion designers – Factor conditions

The existence of world renowned fashion shows in Country L – Related and supporting industries

Fashion conscious customers – Demand conditions

Intense domestic competition – Firm structure, strategy and rivalry

Presence of large number of leather working plants – Related and supporting industries

35   A, C and D

Mitzberg's 5 Ps are:

Ploy

Plan

Position

Perspective

Pattern

36   The correct matching of the definitions is shown below:

Brand competitors	Companies who offer similar products with similar prices.
Industry competitors	Suppliers who produce similar goods but are not necessarily the same size or structure.
Form competitors	Suppliers whose products satisfy the same needs although they are technically quite different.
Generic competitors	Competitors who compete for the same income.

37   B

Logical incrementalism (Quinn) is a positive view of incrementalism whereby the organisation has a clear view of where it wants to go, but it then proceeds towards this goal using small steps. It is prepared to adapt to environmental changes along the way.

Freewheeling opportunism is where an organisation has no real long term plan, instead it may have a series of short-term plans and adapts quickly to the opportunities which present themselves.

Muddling through is another incremental approach in which Lindblom described how Government departments tend to 'muddle through' from year to year rather than carrying out bold strategic initiatives.

Emergent strategy (Mintzberg) is where successful strategies can emerge without formal, deliberate planning. The realised strategy is often made up of partly intended strategy and partly unplanned, emergent strategies.

38   B

This would be the purpose of quantitative research.

39   B

H operates the primary role of Service.

The term 'administration' indicates that S's role is a support activity, as this term is used in the model. The description of his role could only reinforce this conclusion. Likewise, 'information technology' indicates that P performs a support role. Finally, although Porter's term 'procurement' is not included in the statement, Y's responsibilities for dealing with suppliers of inventory and capital equipment are sufficient to conclude that Y also occupies a support role.

40   B

Competitors will need to sell a lot to cover high fixed costs so will fight aggressively to maximise sales and cover their fixed costs.

Rapid growth in the market would actually make existing competition less intense, as existing competitors would struggle to keep up with demand and would not need to acquire competitor's customers to grow.

Relative quality and costs of similar products drives the threat of substitute products.

High barriers to entry would affect the threat of new entrants.

41   B and E

Mission statements address the questions:

- Why do we exist?

- What are we providing?

- For whom do we exist?

42   A

BRIC (Brazil, Russia, India and China) are the world's largest emerging economies.

43   C

Political risk is the possibility of an unexpected politically motivated event in a country affecting the outcome of an investment. Political risk analysis will consider the differences between the home and target country, e.g. the stability of government, the presence of corruption by officials, different religious beliefs or ethnic tensions etc.

44   B

The four conditions proposed by Barney that should be met if resources are to create advantage are: Value, Rarity, Inimitability and Non-substitutability

45 **The correct matching of the definitions is shown below:**

Focused differentiation	Consumers will be willing to pay high prices in this category as they value the uniqueness and exclusivity of the product.
Monopoly pricing	This position can only be achieved where there is only one company in the market or very limited choice for the customer.
Low price	Relies on high volumes to counteract the small margins.
Hybrid	Companies competing here can build up reputation and customer loyalty for offering reasonable goods at fair prices.

46 **A**

Freewheeling opportunism is best used in the early/entrepreneurial stage of the business life cycle. An emergent approach is best used in unpredictable environments where a focus on internal competences might be better than an analysis of the external environment. The rational/formal and incremental approaches would therefore appear to be the best options. The incremental approach is best suited to a situation when the business is still growing and enjoying success. But LMN is maturing and its market has become much more competitive. It needs to analyse the changes in its environment and find a new direction forward. The rational/formal approach will best achieve this.

47 **A, B and E**

C is incorrect as Country risk is a wider, more general risk than political risk. Political risk is a part of country risk.

D is incorrect as political risk can also be indirect. For example due to government policies such as changing interest and exchange rates.

48 **A**

The design (or conception) school is one of the prescriptive schools from the ten listed in the strategy safari and this school believes that strategy development is a rational process which seeks to establish a fit between internal capabilities and external possibilities.

49 **D**

It will be difficult for new companies to enter this market. This is mainly due to the accreditation that is required before a company can offer courses, and this process can take several years.

50 **B and C**

Option A is incorrect in that Big Data does not refer to any specific financial amount. Option D is also incorrect. Big Data can indeed come from many sources, but this is too narrow a definition. Big Data refers to the large volume of data, the many sources of data and the many types of data.

Option F is also incorrect as big data contains both financial and non-financial data.

51   The correct matching is:

- A large cash balance – **Strength**

- A lack of in-house IT expertise – **Weakness**

- A respected and entrepreneurial leader – **Strength**

- Customer resistance to on-line shopping – **Threat**

- Good designs – **Strength**

52   B and D

The existence of patents makes it harder for new companies to enter the market. Also, where the existing firms in the market are large, new starts will find it hard to compete and are therefore less likely to enter the market.

The others would all make it easier or more attractive to enter the market.

53   C and D

Cyert and March suggested four techniques for dealing with stakeholder conflict, these are:

Satisficing – negotiation between the stakeholders

Sequential attention – giving stakeholders turns to realise their objectives

Side Payments – giving some form of compensation to stakeholders whose objectives are not met

Exercise of power – deadlock is overcome by the most powerful stakeholders forcing through their preferred option.

54   C

The highest level of strategy in an organisation is corporate which is decided at the top of the organisation. At this level, fundamental decisions are made such as what industry the business wants to operate in. The second level is business, which looks at how the business will compete in their chosen markets. The final, and lowest, level is operational or functional which looks at the day to day decisions required to support both the business and the corporate strategy.

55   D

PESTEL analyses the macro-environment.

Porter's value chain is an internal analysis of how organisations add value.

Porter's 5 forces is an industrial analysis assessing the ability of an organisation to make profit in a given industry.

Porter's Diamond seeks to answer the question of why certain nations are home to so many internationally successful companies in a given industry.

56 **The completed sentences are:**

Outbound logistics includes distributing the products to customers.

Receiving, storing and handling raw material would come under the heading of **Inbound logistics**.

Procurement would deal with purchasing of raw materials.

Activities involved in the physical creation of the product or the delivery of the service are known as **Primary** activities.

57 **D**

This would be performed after a company has implemented a strategy to evaluate its impact on the business.

58 **C**

Threat of substitutes refers to people's tendency to replace one product with another.

59 **A**

The objective is to prevent this group from joining forces with other, more powerful groups. It is important with this group that the activities of the organisation are presented as rational so that the group gain an understanding as to the reasons behind the organisation's actions.

Minimal effort would be used for stakeholders with low power and low interest.

Keep satisfied would be used for stakeholders with high power and low interest.

Key player would be used for stakeholders with high power and high interest.

60 **B, C and E**

Emergent strategy is not carefully planned by senior management. It is a strategy which adapts to the environment and to the opportunities presented. It is continually changing.

THE HUMAN ASPECTS OF THE ORGANISATION

61   D

The four soft elements of the McKinsey 7s model are staff, skills, style and shared values. The remaining three elements (structure, systems and strategy) are considered hard elements.

62   The correct matching of the definitions is shown below:

The daily behaviours and actions of people that signal acceptable behaviour	Rituals and routines
Who makes the decisions	Power structures
What the organisation is about	The paradigm
The past events and people talked about inside and outside the company	Stories and myths

63   C

With task culture the importance is about getting the job done right and on time

64   The most appropriate action for each of the employees is shown below:

Employee 1	Disciplinary layoff or suspension
Employee 2	An informal talk
Employee 3	An oral warning
Employee 4	Dismissal

65   The correct matching is:

There is one best way to undertake every task – **Taylor's scientific management**

Interpersonal relations are a key part of determining workplace behaviour – **Human relations school**

Managers must control the needs of the task, individual and group – **Adair's action-centred leadership**

Managers can be either a psychologically distant or psychologically close – **Fiedler's contingency theory**

66   A, B and E

Drucker suggested eight key objectives which a business would need to cover all areas where performance and results affect the business. These are: profitability, innovation, market standing, productivity, financial and physical resources, managerial performance and development, worker performance and attitude and public responsibility.

67   C

An effective staff appraisal system can bring many benefits, both to the organisation and to the individual. While it can improve communication, identify training needs and provide a fair process for reward decision, it cannot ensure that performance targets are met.

68   D

High uncertainty avoidance means people are uncomfortable with uncertainty and ambiguity. In these cultures, such as Greece, Japan and Russia, risk taking is generally discouraged and organisations tend to rely heavily on rules regulations.

69   The correct matching is:

A large bureaucratic organisation such as a Government department would likely have this type of culture – **Role culture**

With this type of culture, everything is based on a logical order and rationality – **Role culture**

An organisation which is based on the technical expertise of the individual employees would tend to have this type of culture – **Person culture**

This type of culture would tend to be found in small, owner-run organisations – **Power culture**

70   B

Intrinsic satisfaction is derived from the job content. Extrinsic satisfaction is derived from factors separate to the job itself and is dependent on the decisions of others. Pay, working conditions and benefits are all examples of extrinsic rewards.

71   D

In fact, the manager is actually using legitimate power, because they are only able to promote someone by virtue of their formal authority to do so. Of the options given, however, reward power is the only one that applies: it resides in the manager's ability to influence the subordinate's behaviour by controlling potential promotions (whether or not the subordinate is actually promoted). Referent power is the power to inspire followership in others; to lead by personal charisma.

72   **The complete model is shown below:**

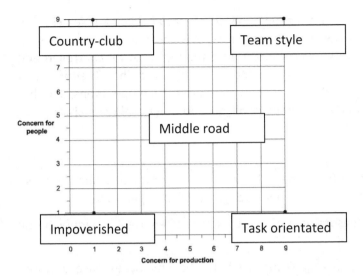

73   **The correct matching is:**

These help to avoid unpleasantness and dissatisfaction – **Hygiene factor**

Good working conditions – **Hygiene factor**

An appropriate level of salary – **Hygiene factor**

Career advancement – **Motivator**

These satisfy the need for personal growth – **Motivator**

74   **C**

Disciplinary action is usually 'progressive': that is, warnings – and subsequent sanctions – become increasingly severe with each failure to adjust performance.

75   **A and B**

A grievance procedure occurs when an employee feels that their superior or colleagues are wrongly treating them.

76   The correct matching is:

Task	Individual maintenance	Group maintenance
• Opinion-seeking	• Feedback	• Peace keeping
• Decision making	• Counselling	• Communicating

77   **B, E and F**

Goals, skills and technology would be a visible elements, but attitudes, style and values would be hidden elements.

78   C

McGregor's Theory X and Theory Y are attitudes based on social science research, and McGregor regarded them as two distinct attitudes. Theory X is based on assumptions such as the dislike of individuals for work, which means that they have to be controlled and threatened by their supervisors and managers. McGregor believed that Theory Y was difficult to apply in some working conditions, such as mass production operations, and that it was much better suited to the management of managers and other professionals.

79   A

Personal centralised control is often found in small, owner-managed organisations. In these organisations, control is carried out by the owner through personal supervision.

Output control is based on the measurement of outputs and is often used in manufacturing organisations.

Clan or cultural control is found in organisations where the employees have a strong identification with management goals and they are given a degree of freedom in how they carry out their tasks.

Bureaucratic control is based on formal rules and procedures and is often found in large hierarchical organisations.

80   C

Managing health and safety is not solely the responsibility of directors. While senior management have a legal requirement to comply with the Health and Safety legislation, all employees also have responsibility towards health and safety.

Managing health and safety in the workplace is a legal requirement in the UK and the requirements are covered by the Health and Safety at work act 1974 (HASAWA).

Cost savings can be made from compliance with health and safety legislation. This comes from lower legal costs for compensation and lower costs due to fewer work days lost by employees.

One of the key areas of the HASAWA is provision of information, training and instruction of staff in areas of health and safety.

81   The correct matching is:

- Its purpose is to remove discrimination – Equal opportunities

- It relies on proactive action – Equal opportunities

- It is a Human Resources role – Equal opportunities

- It is a managerial role – Diversity

82   A and C

Bureaucratic businesses are evidence of high uncertainty avoidance as they give staff defined rules to work with. The fact that junior staff have a say in the running of the business is evidence of low power distance.

83   B

This would be the definition of the role of a mentor.

84   A, D and E

Traditional authority is based on Weber's classical bureaucracy. This is incorrect. Traditional authority is based on custom and practice. Rational-legal authority is based on Weber's classical bureaucracy.

Responsibility is the capacity to exert influence. This is incorrect. This is the definition of power.

85   The complete sentence is:

Under UK law, the director could bring an action for **wrongful** or **unfair** dismissal.

An action for wrongful dismissal is an action for breach of contract of employment: here the contract provides for one year's notice of termination. The director can, alternatively, bring a statutory claim for unfair dismissal under the Employment Rights Act.

86   B

In a task culture, the focus is on getting the job done right and on time. Team work is essential in this culture and in the case if ABC, this is essential if they are to try to compete in their new, more dynamic marketplace. Task culture is the most successful where a company needs to be innovative as innovation often requires cross functional teams.

ABC currently has a role culture where the individual's job description comes first. This is common in large, nationalised industries.

87   D

J's position is clearly unfavourable, with little power and a poor relationship with his staff. Psychologically distant leaders favour formal roles and relationships, judge subordinates on the basis of performance and are primarily task oriented. This would best for J.

In contrast psychologically close leaders do not seek to formalise roles and relationships and are more concerned with maintaining good relationships at work. Their style works best when the situation is moderately favourable.

88   The correct matching of the elements is shown below:

Symbols	There are a finite number of parking spaces allocated to a few key staff members.
Rituals and routines	People often work through lunchtime and it's not unusual for people to work after 6pm.
Control systems	There is a timesheet system accounting for each hour of time worked in a week.
Power structures	All decisions on Audit work programmes come from head office.

89   C

The work of human resources staff is usually hard to quantify, however they have a significant influence on the income a company generates and therefore it is presumed that they should share a part of the profit.

90   A and C

Staff bonuses mean that the manager is offering her staff a reward for adopting the system. She is also relying on referent power by using her charisma/relationship with her employees.

91   C

The Equality Act 2012 covers the following grounds for discrimination:

- Age
- Disability
- Gender reassignment
- Marriage and civil partnership
- Pregnancy and maternity
- Race
- Religion or belief
- Sex
- Sexual orientation

It does not cover discrimination due to physical appearance.

92   C

There is a subtle point here. The delegator must 'back off' in the sense of not constantly checking on or interfering with the subordinate in his or her use of the delegated authority: this would not be genuine delegation at all. However, the point is not to leave the subordinate without guidance or assistance where it may be required: it is important that the delegator be available. The other options are features of effective delegation: note that it is a thoroughly collaborative process.

93   D and E

There are limited grounds for redundancy. Redundancy can occur where a role is no longer required. Roles become redundant and this is not linked to individual conduct or performance. Where there is cessation of a business or part of a business or of certain activities within a business then redundancy can be justified.

94   C

Accountability is about 'answering to' or 'reporting to' more senior. It is an upward requirement. Authority is the 'right' of someone (often by virtue of their position in the hierarchy) to make decisions or give orders. Empowerment is the process whereby greater authority and discretion (and corresponding responsibility) is given to lower levels in the organisation. Super-ordination is a process whereby something is 'higher' than something else in a hierarchy or arrangement: we talk about 'super-ordinate goals', for example, for those at a higher level in the hierarchy of plans.

95   A

There are three levels of control; Strategic, Tactical and Operational.

At the strategic level, the board will set the control environment. Policies for control, such as recruitment, selection, appraisal and discipline will be set.

At the tactical level, the decisions of the board will be implemented. Procedures for controlling recruitment, selection, appraisal and discipline will be established and monitored.

At the operational level, operational controls will be designed to control structured repetitive activities. This could cover activities such as inventory control or ordering systems.

96   C and E

'Values' are the things which can be identified from stories and the opinions of those within the organisation. It includes items such as language used, behaviour and how people justify what they do.

The things that can be seen, heard and observed are 'Artefacts'. Deeply held beliefs are known as 'Basic assumptions' and 'the way we do things around here' is Handy's overall definition of culture.

97   C

Strong cultures can become very set in their ways and as such can affect the organisation's ability to change in light of changes in the environment.

Answers A, B and D are usually seen as advantages of strong cultures.

98   A, B and F

Fayol suggested the five functions of management are Planning, Controlling, Commanding, Co-ordinating and Organising.

99   B, D and E

It is important to remember that responsibility cannot be delegated, but authority must be delegated along with the task in question. Option C is incorrect as the scope of responsibility must correspond to the scope of the authority given. Option F is incorrect as this is the definition of empowerment.

100 A and D

In principle, the more training days an employee receives the more knowledgeable and skilful he or she becomes.

A target for the percentage of total sales revenue earned from new products focuses on innovation. The higher the target percentage, the more innovative the organisation might be with new product development.

MANAGING RELATIONSHIPS

101 B

The indicators in the prompt that confirm G as a completer-finisher include the phrases 'keen eye for detail', identifies minor details in documents that others miss', 'always meets his deadlines' and 'reluctant to involve others'. These are consistent with Belbin's descriptions of the contributions that the completer-finisher can make, as well as possible weaknesses.

Like the completer-finisher, the implementer is disciplined and reliable but is typified by being prepared to take concepts and ideas and then put them into practical effect. The monitor-evaluator considers all alternatives and often displays good judgement, but may lack personal drive. The shaper is good under pressure and challenges the team to achieve its goals.

102 The correct matching is shown below:

Horizontal	Occurs between departments at the same level in the organisation
Vertical	Occurs between individuals and groups at different levels
Constructive	Considered positive and beneficial to the organisation
Destructive	Tends to cause alienation between groups and individuals

103 B

Norming establishes the norms under which the group will operate. This includes how the group will take decisions, behaviour patterns, levels of trust and openness and individual roles.

104 B

The hierarchy solution refers to the situation where the activity is carried out in-house and the market solution refers to the situation when the activity is outsourced.

105 A – Plant

B – Monitor-evaluator

C – Team worker

The plant role is played by a creative individual; the monitor-evaluator is good at making accurate judgements, whereas the team worker looks after the atmosphere within the team.

106 A

This characteristic helps to win positions or gain victories at the other's expense rather than meet the needs of both parties. It is more likely to result in a lose-lose strategy.

107 C, E and F

The finance department can help ensure a profitable selling price is used for EFG's products. Finance will also help set the budget for the sales volume in order to produce the sales budget. They will also provide marketing with information to help determine EFG's market share for various products.

108 A and E

Teams tend to be slower at making decisions than individuals, as there are more people involved in the decision-making process. This also means that decisions are often compromises when made in teams. However, the involvement of more people in the decision making process means that teams have better control – there are a number of people to review the decisions being made.

109 The correct matching is:

This technique involves the conflicting party directly engaging with each other and negotiating with one another to try to work out their differences – **Confrontation**.

This technique involves management imposing shared targets on both parties which will require the cooperation of both parties in order to meet the target – **Superordinate goals**.

With this technique, members of one department will be asked to work in the other department for a period of time, to allow them to better understand the issues faced by the other department – **Member rotation**.

A technique which can be used where conflicting parties are uncooperative is to bring in an independent party to meet with the conflicting parties to encourage them to reach agreement – **Third party consultants**.

110 D

Groupthink involves an unwavering belief in the group and its decisions and a sectarian emphasis on agreement.

The Abilene paradox is a famous case which demonstrates that a group can end up with an outcome that none of the individual members wanted.

Risky shift refers to the tendency for groups to make decisions which are riskier than any of the individual members would take on their own.

Conformity refers to the situation where group members are persuaded by the group to agree with decisions which are obviously wrong, and which they know to be wrong.

111 C

The correct order for the negotiation process is: preparation, opening, bargaining and closing.

112 **The correct matching is shown below:**

A   suppression

B   resolution

C   reduction

D   stimulation and orchestration

Conflict stimulation and orchestration. This approach actively encourages conflict as a means of generating new ideas and new approaches or of stimulating change.

Conflict suppression. This involves the use or threatened use of authority or force, or the avoidance of recognition that a conflict situation exists, or smoothing over the conflict by de-emphasising the seriousness of the situation.

Conflict reduction. This involves building on areas of agreement and on common objectives, and changing attitudes and perceptions of the parties involved.

Conflict resolution. This seeks to eliminate the root causes of conflict by establishing a consensus.

113 **The correct matching is shown below:**

A   **Reciprocity**

B   **Scarcity**

C   **Social proof**

D   **Liking**

Reciprocity – Remind the person of things you have done for them in the past

Social proof – Use the opinions of those already supporting you to influence other to join that support

Scarcity – Advise people that they could lose out if they don't act quickly.

Liking – Building relationships with the people you want to influence so that they trust you.

114 **The correct matching is shown below:**

The assets may be immobile or attached to a particular location	Site
The unique ability to provide a service at a certain time	Temporal
An asset with unique properties	Physical asset
An asset made to an exact specification and has only one application	Dedicated asset

115 **B**

In Belbin's model, it is not necessary for different individuals to carry each role; one person can undertake more than one role. It is just necessary that all the roles are covered.

116 D

In the forming stage, the team comes together. In the next stage (storming), the group reassesses its targets and roles via more or less open conflict. Norming is a period of settling down, where the group establishes norms and ways of working. In the performing stage, the team transfers its energies to task performance. If the team remains for a long time at the performing stage, there is a danger that it can become less effective as it starts to operate on 'automatic pilot'. If this happens it is best to adjourn the group.

117 The completed sentences are:

When the finance function is carried out by an external party, this is known as **Business Process Outsourcing**.

With **Business Process Outsourcing** the confidentiality risk is **increased**.

Reduced premises costs and **increased** quality of service provision are benefits of **Shared services centres**.

With **Business partnering** the knowledge of the business area is **increased** but there can be duplication of effort across the organisation.

118 C

A win:win approach which seeks to benefit all parties is known as collaborating. This approach is used when there is high assertiveness and high cooperativeness. The goal with compromising is to find a middle ground, however this can be seen as a 'lose-lose' since neither party gets what it really wants. Competing is a 'win-lose' approach and accommodating is a 'lose-win' approach.

119 B

The way words are said can be more important than the actual words themselves.

120 D

This is the definition of negotiation.

121 The correct matching is shown below:

Plant	Imaginative and very good at coming up with original ideas and suggestions.
Completer Finisher	Gives attention to detail and is concerned with meeting deadlines.
Team Worker	Supports other members of the team and helps to promote harmony.

122 A and D

Mainwaring suggested four conflict managing strategies: suppression, resolution, reduction and stimulation and orchestration.

123 D

Norming means agreeing who should be doing what and establishing modes of behaviour, with team relationships becoming settled. The project manager will begin to pass control and authority for decision-making to the team members.

124 C

There are 6 types of asset specificity; site, physical, human asset, brand name, dedicated and temporal.

125 A

The shaper is described as someone who is committed to the task, may be aggressive and challenging, will always promote activity. The plant is the thoughtful and thought-provoking individual, the team worker is concerned with the relationships within the group, and the completer finisher is the progress chaser who ensures deadlines are met.

126 The correct order is shown below:

1	Preparation
2	Opening
3	Bargaining
4	Closing

127 A and D

Vaill suggested the following five characteristics were shared by high performance teams.

- Clarification of broad purposes and short term objectives.
- Commitment to purposes.
- Teamwork focused on the task at hand.
- Strong and clear leadership.
- Generation of inventions and new methods.

128 C

Advisors can be contacted in many situations and may be equally useful when the organisation is doing well as when it is doing badly.

129 **The correct matching is shown below:**

Conformity	Individuals within the group can be persuaded to accept decisions which they know to be wrong
Abilene paradox	The group can end up with an outcome which none of the members wanted
Risky shift	Groups can end up taking decisions which are riskier than the individual members would take
Groupthink	Group members reach consensus without critically testing, analysing and evaluating ideas

130 **C**

Synergy is often described as 2+2=5.

131 **The complete sentences are:**

Where boundaries between departments are not clearly defined, this can cause problems of **interdependencies**.

Communication problems can lead to **misunderstandings**.

History suggests that conflict tends to be self-perpetuating.

132 **The correct matching is shown below:**

What is being transmitted	Message
The medium through which the message is being sent	Channel
The message is translated and its meaning is generated	Decoding
The receiver responds to the message	Feedback
Anything which stops the message being transmitted as intended	Noise

133 **A, B and C – Horizontal**

D – Vertical

Horizontal conflict occurs between groups or departments at the same level in the organisation while vertical conflict occurs at different levels of the organisation.

134 **A** **Reciprocity**

B **Liking**

C **Social proof**

Reciprocity means identifying what you want to achieve and what you need from the other person then considering what you may be able to offer them in return.

Liking means building relationships with those you want to influence so that they trust you.

Social proof means using the opinions of those already supporting you to influence others to join that support.

135 C

Non-verbal actions can vary between countries and cultures.

136 A   Business process outsourcing (BPO)

B   Business partnering

C   Shared services centre (SSC)

Business process outsourcing (BPO) – The finance function is carried out by an external party

Business partnering – A dedicated finance function is set up within each business unit

Shared services centre (SSC) – The finance function is consolidated and run as a central unit within the organisation

137 The correct matching is shown below:

Attendees talk too much	Chairperson should impose order
Objectives of the meeting are unclear	Agenda should be circulated before the meeting
Action points from previous meetings not carried out	Ensure action points agreed and minutes of meeting are issued
Lack of enthusiasm at the meeting	Ensure the correct attendees are invited

138 C

Persuasion is a stronger form of influence.

Persuasion is always direct.

Persuasion falls short of telling the other person what to do, the aim is to get their agreement.

139 D

BPOs will generally carry out finance function for many organisations therefore they tend to develop best practice.

Using BPO can cause the organisation to lose control as it will be harder for them to dictate the information they need and when they need it.

BPO generally results in cost reduction through economies of scale.

D is correct. With BPO, the third party will require access to a considerable amount of confidential information.

140 C

Conflict reduction involves building on areas of agreement and on common objectives, and changing attitudes and perceptions of the parties involved. Techniques that can be used include compromises and concessions. These can be facilitated by independent third party interventions, such as conciliation and arbitration.

MANAGING CHANGE THROUGH PROJECTS

141 A

An internal trigger for change is an event or development within the organisation itself, rather than a change that is started by external developments. Changes in fashion trends, environmental legislation and demands for a shorter working week are all examples of external triggers for change, caused by technological, political or social change.

142 The correct matching is shown below:

Work packages and Statements of work	To specify the work to be done for each activity and who will carry it out
Cost breakdown structure	To cost each element of the project
Work breakdown structure	To divide the work to be carried out into manageable pieces
Product breakdown structure	To identify the product purchases required for each activity

143 C

Don't confuse 'configuration management' (tracking changes to project products, and hence product versions) and 'conformance management' (using inspection, quality control and quality assurance to ensure that the product/service meet the customer's specifications and requirements). While configuration management is also part of 'change management', this term implies a wider process of dealing with the need to amend projects in line with changes in user requirements, or difficulties of realising them in practice.

144 A

The first stage of the project life cycle (identification of a need) involves identifying a need, opportunity or problem. During this stage a feasibility study will be carried out. At the end of this phase the company will decide whether to proceed with the project, and if it does a PID (project initiation document) will be produced.

145 A and D

Driving forces are the forces for change, and restraining forces are the factors resistant to change. To achieve desired change, management should recognise what the key driving and restraining forces are. In principle, change can be achieved either by making the driving forces stronger or the restraining forces weaker. Lewin argued that in practice, it is more effective to reduce the strength of the main restraining forces.

146 **The correct matching is shown below:**

Resource histogram	Helps with capacity planning
Critical path analysis	Identifies the activities that cannot overrun without delaying the overall project completion
PERT	Allows a calculation of contingency to be added to the project plan
Breakdown structures	Establishes the authority and responsibility for each part of the project

147 **A**

In the unfreezing stage, managers need to make the need for change so obvious that most people can easily understand and accept it. Unfreezing also involves creating the initial motivation to change by convincing staff of the undesirability of the present situation.

148 **A**

Kanter suggested that change-adept organisations share the following attributes:

- effective leaders who encourage the development of new concepts – imagination to innovate

- leaders who provide competence both personally and in the organisation as a whole – professionalism to perform

- leaders who make connections with and collaborate with 'partners' outside the organisation – openness to collaborate.

149 **C**

In the PRINCE2 project organisational structure, the project assurance team fulfils this role. The project committee is also representative of user, executive and supplier interests, but its task is to provide senior input to project management. Project support is an optional set of administrative roles.

150 **The correct matching is shown below:**

1   Initiating

2   Planning

3   Controlling

4   Executing

5   Closing

151 **B**

The project steering committee is ultimately responsible for closing down a project. This may happen at the recommendation of the project manager.

152 C

The question defines a 'Work Breakdown Structure' (WBS). CBS is a Cost Breakdown Structure (a similar approach, but applied to costs rather than tasks). CPA is Critical Path Analysis. PID is a project initiation document which is the output of the initiating phase of the project.

153 D

As this involves radical change implemented in a short period of time this would be a revolutionary change.

154 D

The scope of the project explains the boundaries of the project and exactly what is going to be delivered.

155 C

A project manager requires many skills, including negotiation, leadership, change management and problem solving amongst others but the project manager does not usually require specialist financial skills. Accountants involved in the project can provide these skills.

156 D

The team have been together for time and work successfully together. They respect C as the team leader. This suggests that the team are working at the performing stage of team development.

The completed CPA for the project is:

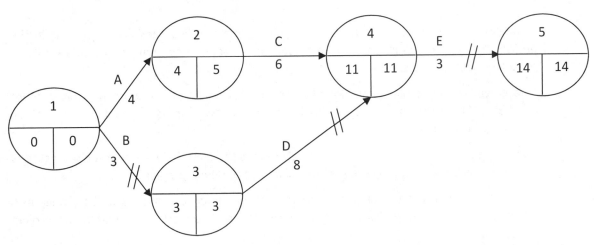

157   The overall project duration is **14 months**

158   **B – the critical activities are B, D and E**

159   D

Beer and Nohria argued in favour of a 'balanced approach', combining concern for economic value (such as reducing the size of the workforce, restructuring or incentive schemes) and concern for human capabilities and the learning process. Using one approach followed by the other will be much less effective in introducing change successfully.

160   D

The project sponsor makes the yes/no decisions about the project, is responsible for approving the project plan and provides the funding for the project. The project manager reports project progress to the project sponsor.

161   B

The other changes are all major 'transformational' changes that affect the organisation's culture and way of operating.

162   B

A resource histogram is a component bar chart showing the number and mix of resources required each day (or other time unit) for the duration of a project.

A Gantt chart is a horizontal bar chart, where the length of the bar represents duration of an activity (whether planned or actual duration, or both, for comparison).

A network diagram is used to present the activities required for the project using arrows and nodes. It shows which activities must be done before others and highlights where activities can be delayed or done at the same time as other activities.

A work breakdown structure breaks down a project into manageable pieces and is an important starting point for planning a project.

163   B

A milestone is used to assess the status of the project. Milestones are key points in the project life cycle which give the project sponsor or steering committee an opportunity to review project progress.

A gate, which may also be a milestone, is a specific review point in the project which cannot be passed unless the performance of the project to that point has met predetermined performance standards.

A critical path is the chain of events that determines the overall duration of the project. Any delays to any activity on the critical path will delay the whole project.

PERT stands for project evaluation and review technique and this is a technique used alongside critical path analysis to attempt to overcome uncertainties within the project time plan.

164   D

Technical feasibility investigates whether project requirements can be met using available material, technology and processes: i.e. is it possible? Economic feasibility investigates whether there will be a benefit that outweighs the cost: i.e. is it worthwhile? Social feasibility investigates whether the project fits with the culture and social organisation of the firm: i.e. *can* our people do this? Ecological feasibility investigates whether the project is environmentally sound and sustainable: i.e. *should* we do this?

165   A, B and D

The Project Management Body of Knowledge (PMBoK) describes nine key areas:

- Integration
- Scope
- Time
- Cost
- Quality
- Human Resources
- Communications
- Risk
- Procurement

166   A

Matrix structures have a number of advantages when used in companies which run a number of projects. It can improve lateral communication and cooperation between specialists as decision making needs to cut across divisional boundaries.

B is incorrect as matrix structures can make reporting to managers more difficult due to the fact that employees can become confused by reporting to two mangers.

C is incorrect as matrix structures can lead to increased time spent in meetings as mangers need to discuss the prioritising of tasks.

D is incorrect as the matrix structure is most useful where a company runs a number of projects but where the projects have different start and end dates as the matrix structure can make it easier to reassign resources between projects.

167   C

There are 6 process areas in PRINCE2:

- Starting up a project
- Initiation
- Managing stage boundaries
- Controlling a stage
- Managing product delivery
- Project closure

168 A

A project sponsor usually makes key 'yes/no' decisions and provides the resources for a project.

The project manager is responsible for the successful delivery of the project objectives.

The project owner is the person for whom the project is being carried out.

The project customer (or user) is the person, or group of people, whose needs the project is attempting to satisfy.

169 A   Senior user

      B   Project manager

      C   Stage team leader

      D   Project assurance team

The completed diagram is shown below:

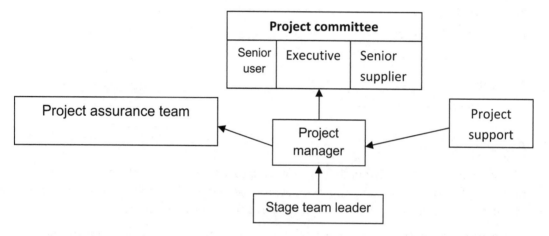

This is a useful diagram: note which way the reporting/authority arrows point. The project manager is the interface between the project committee (or board) and the stage team leaders. The project assurance team provides an independent 'lateral' view of how the project is progressing, reflecting the interests of the committee members. The project support roles provide administrative and communication activities.

170 C

A,B and D would all normally be include in the final report. The extent to which the benefits defined in the original business case have been achieved (C) would not normally be included in the final report as this would not be able to be ascertained until a few months after the completion of the project.

171 A

Unfreezing is the process of both getting employees to recognise that the current situation is unsatisfactory, and also identifying a better way of doing things. Getting qualified staff to accept that some of their work can be done by trained but unqualified people would be a part of the unfreezing process.

172 D

Perhaps this is the obvious solution. Answer B implies no change at all. Attempts to impose change are likely to end in failure, and answers A and C are both incorrect. A change culture within an organisation has to start with top management, who must give their full support and encouragement to change programmes.

173 The float time on activity C is **8 days**

The completed CPA is shown below:

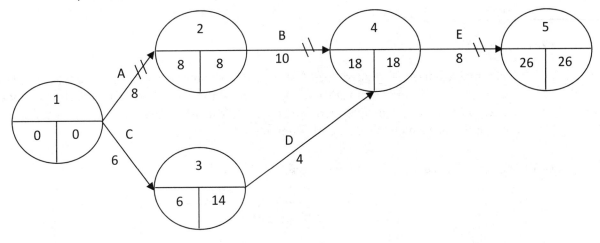

The float time is calculated as: Latest event time minus Earliest event time. For C this would be: 14 − 6 = 8 days

The critical path activities (A, B, E) have a zero float.

174 B

The scope of the project explains what should be included in the project deliverables. This has to be agreed at the outset of the project before detailed planning takes place.

175 B

Change in most organisations is triggered by changes in their external environment rather than internal developments. The external changes might affect the organisation's culture and will eventually prompt management action (answers A and D). The trigger for change, however, comes from the external environment.

176 The completed sentences are:

A change that aims to allow the business to maintain its current market share by adopting minor initiatives over the next few years would be known as **adaptation**.

A change that is implemented gradually through inter-related initiatives is known as **evolution**.

177 D

Progress reporting is a control activity which should be carried out regularly by the project manager. The other items (A, B and C) would all specifically be included in configuration management.

178 B

Satisficing is a method suggested by Cyert and March for dealing with conflicting stakeholder objectives. The aim with satisficing is to keep as many stakeholders as possible happy.

179 C

Team management is graded (9, 9). The other options are Country Club (1, 9), Task orientated (9, 1) and Impoverished (1, 1). Note that, in Blake and Mouton's model, concerns for task and people were not mutually exclusive: the 'best' style, according to them, is to have a high focus on both elements.

180 The completed diagram is shown below:

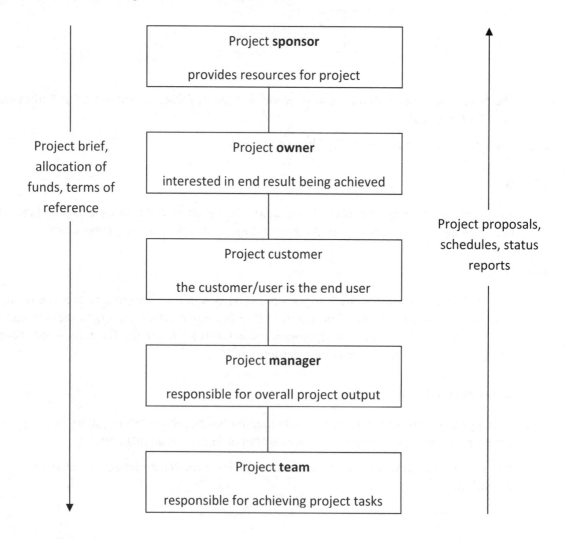

181 D

The carrying out of risk analysis is carried out as part of the initiating stage of the project lifecycle.

The other activities (A, B and C) would all be carried out during the executing stage.

182 The correct matching is:

A change that is to be implemented over a long period of time but will radically alter the business operations – **Evolution**

A change to realign the way in which the organisation operates, implemented in a series of small steps – **Adaptation**

A change to realign the way in which the organisation operates, with many initiatives being implemented simultaneously – **Reconstruction**

Transformational change that occurs via simultaneous initiatives on many fronts – **Revolution**

183 C

Tuckman suggested that all teams go through the following stages of development:

- Forming
- Storming
- Norming
- Performing
- Adjourning

At the norming stage, standards of working are established and ways of working are agreed.

184 D

A Gantt chart is a horizontal bar chart with the length of each bar representing the length of the activity.

185 C

Conformance management is concerned with compliance with technical specifications and would focus on items such as inspection, quality control and quality assurance.

Focus on items such as prioritising change requests, recording of changes and agreement of a change budget would suggest a change process.

Focus on items such as functional quality and client satisfaction measures would suggest a performance management system.

Focus on items such as access control over project records and version control for documentation would suggest configuration management.

186 A, B and C

The main control elements used within projects are project meetings and project reports. The feasibility study is produced at the initiation stage of the project to help management decide on whether the project is worth undertaking. Scenario planning is used at the planning stage of the project to consider the risk and uncertainty within the project.

187 C

The external review is an important review carried out at the end of the project. It is a review held with the customer to establish if the project had satisfied customer requirements.

Progress reports are an important technique used during the controlling of the project.

Gantt charts are used in planning the time requirements of the project during the planning stage.

PERT is used to take account of uncertainty and risk during the planning stage.

188 B

Progress review meetings should be regular, formal meetings involving the project manager, team members and the customer or steering committee. The purpose of these meetings is to provide an update on the project status and to identify any issues and action plans from that point.

Team meetings should also be held regularly between the project manager and the project team members. The object of these meetings is to keep all team members up to date with project progress.

Problem solving meetings are held on an ad hoc basis to deal with specific problems which have arisen in the project.

Business review meetings are held at the end of the project as part of the overall review of the project.

189 D

The identification of need phase incorporates initiation. Note that scheduling is part of the planning phase, milestone reviews are part of implementation and control, and completion happens at the end of the lifecycle.

190 C

The critical path can be identified from the nodes. Where the earliest event time (EET) and the latest event time (LET) are the same, this indicates that there is no 'slack' in these activities and therefore the activities are on the critical path.

191 B, C and E

The slack on activities C and F is 13 weeks.

Activities A, B and C can start straight away. Activity D cannot start until after activity A is complete.

192 C

Risks with high likelihood and low impact are best managed by reduction. Reduction of risk can be achieved by implementing controls, or by taking alternative courses of action.

Risks with high likelihood and high impact should be avoided.

Risks with low likelihood and high impact should be transferred.

Risks with low likelihood and low impact should be accepted.

193 B

Buffering involves adding artificial slack into risky activities. It adds padding to the original estimates and allows for the fact that it is difficult to ensure that all stages and activities are carried out exactly as planned.

Scenario planning is another technique which can be used to take account of risk and uncertainty in projects. This involves the considering of one or more sets of circumstances that might occur within the project other than the most likely or expected set of circumstances.

Float refers to the extra time available for project activities which are not in the critical path.

PERT (project evaluation and review technique) uses a formula to calculate an expected time for each activity, taking into account a probable time, an optimistic time and a pessimistic time.

194 D

Contingency theory suggests that the effectiveness of various managerial practices, styles and techniques will vary according to the particular circumstances of the situation. The contingency theorists embrace any and all appropriate principles that enable managers to manage more effectively. Regardless of the organisational structure or the obstacles and opportunities they encounter, managers have some leeway in the choices they make and in the actions they initiate and they should be able to adapt their actions to suit the situation.

195 A

In the theory X model, people are seen as lazy and will work only if there is a direct link between efforts and rewards. A Theory Y manager would consider that all of the other factors would motivate.

196 A, C and E

Project management software is very useful and can make the management of projects easier. B is incorrect as the software can help in managing the time in the project but cannot ensure that the project meets its deadline.

D is also incorrect as project management software is generally inexpensive and may be no more complex than standard office software.

197   B

Fear of more monotonous work, concern over feeling less valued and feeling that the change suggests criticism of current performance would all come under personal factors.

198   A, B and E

C is incorrect. The matrix structure is commonly used in many industries, especially engineering, construction and consulting.

D is incorrect. The matrix structure is most useful where organisations regularly carry out multiple projects.

199   A and D

The strategies for managing resistance to change as defined by Kotter and Schlesinger are:

- Participation

- Education and communication

- Power/coercion

- Facilitation and support

- Manipulation and co-optation

- Negotiation

200   A, C and D

Herzberg's model states that a number of factors should be put in place in order to avoid dissatisfaction. These are known as hygiene factors. Once hygiene factors are in place, motivational factors can be put in place. B and E are motivational factors. These factors will increase motivation as long as the hygiene factors are already in place.

This is an important consideration for a project manager who must try to motivate the project team.